HANDBOOK OF
WINNING
POKER

ABOUT THE AUTHOR

Edwin Silberstang is acknowledged by the top professionals in the gambling world as the leading authority on games in America. His first book, *Playboy's Book of Games*, published in 1972, was an instant best seller and a selection of the Book of the Month Club. That classic work is now republished by Cardoza Publishing as *Silberstang's Encyclopedia of Games and Gambling*.

Since then, Silberstang has published over thirty books dealing with games, gambling and the Vegas scene. His expertise has been used in the entertainment world, and he was the technical adviser on the film, *Big Town*, a story about a young gambler starring Matt Dillon, produced by Columbia Pictures.

In addition, he has written and starred in his own videos about gambling, and has appeared on many television and radio shows throughout the country. He is constantly called upon as a consultant and teacher as well.

Silberstang's success in the field of gambling writing comes from a skill as a novelist combined with a vast knowledge of gambling. His writing is clear and concise and he not only is able to present information but to make it interesting and fascinating.

Now he brings his expertise to poker, a field he has mastered, where his solid knowledge of the game has been acknowledged by world champions and other legendary figures of the game.

HANDBOOK OF
WINNING POKER

Edwin Silberstang

CARDOZA PUBLISHING

For My Sister Phyllis

Cardoza Publishing, publisher of **Gambling Research Institute** (GRI) books, is the foremost gaming publisher in the world with a library of more than 50 up-to-date and easy-to-read books and strategies. These authoritative works are written by the top experts in their fields and with more than 5,000,000 books in print, represent the best-selling and most popular gaming books anywhere.

First Cardoza Edition   January 1996

Library of Congress Catalog Card No: 95-74916
ISBN: 0-940685-60-4
Front Cover Photo By Denise De Luise, Author Photo by Carole Donovan

CARDOZA PUBLISHING
P.O. Box 1500, Cooper Station, New York, NY 10276
Phone (718)743-5229 • Fax (718) 743-8284

Write for your free catalogue of gambling books,
advanced strategies, and computer items.

Table of Contents

1. INTRODUCTION

Poker is a fascinating and exciting card game because it combines the elements of skill, luck, and psychological insight. There is no other game quite like it, and it has become the most popular of American card games.

It is a game that can be played at a casino, poker club, or at home, but no matter where it is played, the principles and strategies are the same. This is so because it is a game that is not played against a house or casino but against other players.

Poker is, above all, a money game, which can be played for high or low stakes. So we not only have a game in which skill, luck, and psychology play a part, but one in which the discerning player can use his insight to make money.

Make no mistake about it, poker is primarily a gambling game and can be played for pennies or for thousands of dollars, depending on the circumstances and the bankrolls of the players. And whether played as a penny-ante game or for unlimited stakes, the game retains its high level of excitement.

What separates poker from many other card games is that it is pliable rather than rigid. During the course of a session or evening many variations of poker can be played at the same table.

If the players agree to "dealer's choice", each dealer can determine what game will be played while he has the deal, and the poker variations are many. To list some: There is high draw poker, either jackpots or anything opens; or low draw, called lowball; five-card, six-card, and seven-card stud; and all these stud games can be played as high or low. There is high-low poker, hold'em, and any of the crisscross games. And within these games are still more variations, such as a wild card or wild joker, blind bet and live blind bet, roll your own - the list goes on and on.

It is, in addition to all that I have written, a game of expectations and a game in which one must be patient, waiting for events to occur. In all poker games the conclusion is never final after the player is dealt his initial cards. In some variations he draws cards; in others, particularly in the stud games, he buys cards round after round; in still other variations he shares common cards with other players, cards that are placed face up on the board.

In all these games bets are made on every round and may be raised and reraised, adding to the excitement. Also, in all poker variations some or all of the cards dealt to the players are closed or hidden cards, and within these hidden cards lie the mystery and fascination of poker.

There is yet one more feature that makes this game so popular. A player is never really stuck with his hand to the bitter end. He always has the option of folding or dropping out of play. It is not like most other gambling card games in which one must play on and on no matter how bad the cards. In poker, a player can get out without giving up money, and in this one special feature rests much of the skill of poker. The most important consideration in any variation is when to stay in and when to get out of the game. It will be discussed at length during the course of this book.

A unique feature of poker is the bluff. A "bluff" may be defined as a large bet on a hand that is not the strongest, with the intention of driving the other players out of the game. In poker, if you get all the other players out of the game, you can win the pot even with a poor hand.

To bluff successfully, indeed, to play a winning game, you must study your opponents and the psychology of the game. For someone who can do this well, and who can learn the skills involved, poker pays off with wins and big money.

What you do when you play poker is to test not only skill of your opponents but also their insight and courage. Boldness and courage are important elements, and they come with confidence and knowledge of the game. You must know when to bluff, when to stay in, when to raise, how to read other hands, how to tell when your opponent is bluffing - in other words, all the necessary skills.

Having these skills will make you a winning player. Poker, no matter what most people think, is primarily a game of skill. The purpose of this book is to show you what you must know to acquire that skill. First, it will teach you the game of poker; the fundamentals and basics. Then, as you learn these, you will learn, step by step, both basic and advanced strategies. By the time you finish this book, you should be able not only to hold your own in any game you enter but also, with experience, to win on a regular basis.

Becoming a winner at poker can pay off very well, in fun, self-confidence, and, of course, in money. Read this book, study it well, and you'll end up a winner in one of the most fascinating games known, a game that will give you hours of pleasure as well as tremendous profits.

2. FUNDAMENTAL RULES OF POKER

The Deck

The standard 52-card deck is used for poker. The 52 cards are divided into four suits; spades ♠, hearts ♥, diamonds ♦, and clubs ♣. None of the suits has precedence over any other suit. Each suit consists of 13 cards, in the following rank: Ace is the highest, followed by the king, queen, jack, 10, 9, 8, 7, 6, 5, 4, 3, and finally the 2, the lowest-ranking card.

The ace is unique in that it sets the boundaries of hands. It may be used as the highest card, such as in a straight consisting of ace, king, queen, jack, and 10. Any flush in which an ace appears is called an ace-high flush. For example, holding all spades consisting of ace, jack, 9, 7, and 4, the ace would be the highest ranking card, and the hand would be an "ace-high" flush.

The ace can also be used as the lowest-ranking card to form a low straight. For example, holding 5, 4, 3, 2, and ace of varying suits, you would hold a 5-high straight. In this instance, as well as in the low poker games, the ace is the lowest-ranking card in the deck.

To repeat, the ace can either be the lowest or the highest card in any straight. However, a hand such as jack, queen, king, ace, and 2 is not a straight, and neither is a hand of king, ace, 2, 3, and 4. To form a straight with an ace holding, the ace must be either the lowest or the highest card in that straight and form the boundaries of the straight.

These hands will be studied in fuller detail in the discussion of ranks of hands, but, remember that for the present, in all examples but one, the low straight, the ace is the highest-ranking card in any hand.

Object of the Game

In any poker hand, the object of the game is to win the pot. The pot is the accumulated money bet during all the rounds that have taken place in a particular game of poker.

A player can win the pot in either of two ways. First, and most usual, he holds the best hand of those hands remaining at the end of play, which is called the "showdown". For example, in high draw or stud, if one player holds three 4s, that hand beats a hand consisting of three 2s; thus, the higher-ranking hand of three 4s wins the pot.

The second way a pot can be won is by forcing all of the competition out of the game prior to the showdown, so that you alone remain in. At that point you can claim the pot and collect the winnings.

To repeat: One wins the game and the pot by having the best hand at the showdown or by forcing out all the other players prior to the showdown.

What if two hands at the showdown are of equal rank? If they are identical in rank and value, the two players split the pot between them.

Rank of the Hands - High Poker

The rank of the hands in high poker is in a predetermined order, based on the law of probability. Since the most difficult or least probable hand to get is a royal flush, which consists of ace, king, queen, jack, and ten of one suit, it is the highest-ranking hand, using the 52-card deck and no wild cards.

Before going further into this ranking, I will digress for a moment and discuss wild cards. In most forms of poker no card is considered wild. However, in some variations a card such as a joker or a 2 may be declared wild.

A "wild card" has any designation, value, rank, or suit that a player desires to give it. For example, if deuces are wild, and you hold four clubs and are dealt the 2 of diamonds, you may designate it as the ace of clubs.

Where there is a wild card, the highest ranking of all hands is five of a kind. Suppose you are dealt four queens and a joker, which is wild. That wild card can now be turned into a fifth queen.

Since most game are not played with wild cards, we will now show the relative ranking of all hands in poker, in descending order.

Royal Flush

In all games in which no wild card is used, a royal flush is absolutely the highest ranking of all hands. It consists of the ace, king, queen, jack, and 10 of one suit. Example ♥ A ♥ K ♥ Q ♥ J ♥ 10.

In poker no suits take precedence over any other, so in the unlikely event that two players hold a royal flush, the pot would be split.

Straight Flush

This is the second-highest ranking of all hands. It consists of five cards of *one* suit in continuous sequence, such as ♣ 8 ♣ 7 ♣ 6 ♣ 5 ♣ 4. Another example is ♠ 5 ♠ 4 ♠ 3 ♠ 2 ♠ A.

When two players hold a straight flush, the player holding the highest-ranking card in the flush beats out the other player. For example, if one player held queen, jack, 10, 9, and 8 of hearts, and the other player held jack, 10, 9, 8, 7, and 6 of spades, the straight flush headed by the queen, which is a higher-ranked card than the jack, would win the pot.

If both players held identically ranked cards, the pot would be split.

Four of a Kind

This is the third-highest ranking hand in poker and consists of four cards of equal rank, one from each suit. For example, the ♠ 6 ♥ 6 ♦ 6 ♣ 6 constitutes a four of a kind hand. The fifth card in these hands is immaterial since there can be no ties among four of a kind hands.

When two or more players hold four of a kind hands, the one holding the highest-ranked four of a kind wins the pot. Four kings are higher than four queens, four 10s beat out four 9s, etc.

Full House

In this hand there are two groupings of cards, a three of a kind and a pair. The following are full houses: 888 JJ: KKK AA: 444 99; 999 44.

In determining the winner of the pot when two or more players hold full houses, the hand holding the higher-ranked three of a kind wins the pot. There are no ties in full-house hands.

If one player holds 222 AA, and the other holds KKK 33, the king-high hand wins since that rank in three of a kind beats out the deuces in the other three of a kind holding within the full house. The pairs don't matter in terms of ranking full houses.

The common method of calling out a full house is to announce the three-of-a-kind hand and the word "full." To illustrate, if a player holds 999 JJ, he announces that he has "nines full"; 333 AA would be "threes full."

Flush

Any five cards in *one* suit, not in consecutive sequence, is a flush. For example ♣ K ♣ Q ♣ 8 ♣ 5 ♣ 4 would be called a "king-high" flush. Likewise, the cards ♥ J ♥ 5 ♥ 4 ♥ 3 ♥ 2 would be a "jack-high" flush.

When two or more players have flushes, the one with the highest-ranking card heading the flush wins the pot. An ace in a flush is always the highest-ranking card. An ace-high flush beats out a king-high flush, a 9-high flush beats out an 8-high flush, etc.

It may be possible that two players at a showdown have flushes headed by a card of equal rank. For example, both players may announce a "jack-high" flush. When that occurs, the second ranked card determines the winner. Should one player hold J, 8, 7, 4, 2 of clubs, and the other hold J, 7, 6, 5, 2 of diamonds, the "jack 8" flush would beat out the "jack 7" flush. If both players had identically ranked first and second high cards, then the third card is used, and if the first three are identical, then the fourth is used to determine the winner, down to the fifth card.

Should all five cards in each flush be identical in rank, which is of course unlikely, the pot is split.

Straight

A straight consists of any five cards in consecutive sequence but not of the same suit. ♣ 10 ♣ 9 ♦ 8 ♣ 7 ♣ 6 is a straight but not a straight flush since the diamond 8 prevents that. Another example of a straight is ♠ Q ♦ J ♦ 10 ♥ 9 ♣ 8.

An ace in a straight is always either the highest- or lowest-ranking card. For example, ♠ A ♣ K ♣ Q ♦ J ♥ 10 is an ace-high straight, while ♦ 5 ♦ 4 ♠ 3 ♥ 2 ♠ A is a 5-high straight, the ace having the equivalent value of a 1.

An ace sets the boundaries of a straight. Unless it is the lowest- or highest-ranking card, it cannot be used in a straight. ♣ 2 ♦ A ♥ K ♥ Q ♠ J is not a straight.

The highest ranking of straights wins the pot when two or more players hold straights. A 10-high straight is better than a 9-high straight, and an ace-high straight is always the best straight.

Should both players at a showdown hold identical straights the pot is split.

Three of a Kind

This hands consists of three cards of equal rank, along with two odd cards. An example would be 555 AQ, or 999 43.

There can be no ties in three of kind hands, which are sometimes called triplets. The hand holding the highest-ranked three of a kind hand wins the pot

Two Pair

When a player holds two separate pairs of equally ranked cards, he is said to have "two pair." Examples of this would be KK 22 and 99 33. The fifth card is always odd. The first hand would be called "kings over deuces," "Kings and deuces," or "Kings up."

If two or more players hold two-pair hands, the highest ranking of the pairs would win. "Queens up" beats "jacks up." Should both players have equally ranked high pairs, then the second pair's rank determines the winner of the pot.

For example, 77 33 beats 77 22. Should both pairs be identical, such as 99 44 and 99 44, then the odd fifth card's rank determines the winner of the pot; 99 44 7 beats 99 44 6. Should all five cards be identical in rank, the pot is split.

One Pair

This hand consists of a single pair and three odd cards. The following are examples of one pair hands: 88 AQ5, 99 J73, QQ 987.

Should two players have one-pair hands, which is common, the highest ranking of the pairs wins the pot. For example, a pair of 9s beats out a pair of 8s; a pair of queens beats out a pair of jacks; and a pair of aces beats out any other pair.

Should two players have equally ranked pairs, the highest ranking of the odd cards determines the winner of the pot. Should both the pairs and the highest odd card be equal, the next highest ranking card determines the winner of the pot. Thus, 88 A94 beats out 88 A86.

Should all five cards be identical or equal in rank, the pot is split.

No Pairs

This hand consists of five odd cards, neither in sequence or of one suit, and is the lowest ranking of all hands. ♠ K ♦ Q ♥ 10 ♥ 6 ♠ 5 is an example of a no-pairs hand. Another example is ♣ K ♦ J ♠ 8 ♠ 4 ♠ 2.

When two or more players have no-pairs hands, the player holding the highest-ranking odd card wins the pot. Should two players hold equally ranked high odd cards, the second highest-ranked card determines the winner, and if these are equal, the third card, and so on, until a winner is determined. Thus, K J 9 8 4 beats out K J 9 8 3. If all five cards are equal in rank, the pot is split.

One final word: When discussing hands of equal strength, we are assuming that these hands are the highest-ranked hands at the showdown. For example, if two players have flushes and another a straight, since the flushes are higher than the straight, the holder of the highest-ranking card among the flushes would win the pot.

But should one player hold a flush and two players hold a straight, since the flush is of a higher rank than the straights, the flush hand wins the pot automatically.

The Deal

In private games one of the players deals the cards to the other players. In the Nevada casinos a house dealer has that duty, and none of the players gets the opportunity to deal the cards. In poker clubs, depending upon the state, the dealer's duty will be performed by either the players, in turn, or by a home dealer.

In all private games and in club games where players take turns acting as the dealer each player at the table gets the deal as it moves around the table in clockwise order. Holding the dealer's position is a definite advantage in games like draw poker and hold'em, in which the dealer bets and acts last.

In the stud-poker games the dealer has no advantage because either the high-card or low-card will open, depending on the game.

Dealer's Duties

The dealer must shuffle the cards thoroughly, then, after they are cut by the player to his right, deal them out one at a time to the players in the game.

In draw poker he will deal all of the cards "closed", that is, face down. In stud poker some cards will be dealt open and some closed. The dealer is responsible for each player, including himself, getting the right number of cards.

In stud poker the dealer calls the high card or hand on board (showing) to determine who makes the opening bet on any round of play, and he must make certain that the betting is in proper sequence and that the amount bet is correct.

In draw poker he must make sure that all the players have anted, that the ante is correct, that the betting is in correct sequence, and that all bets are correct. After the draw he must gather in all the discards and deal out the right number of cards to each player. Then he must make certain that the proper player opens the second betting round, that all bets are correct again, and that the sequence of betting is in the proper order.

Betting Rounds

In practically all poker variations there is more than one betting round. In draw poker there are two: one before the draw and one after the draw.

In hold'em there are four betting rounds: one before the flop, one after, one on Fourth Street, and one on Fifth Street.

In stud poker the betting rounds vary according to the game. In five-card stud there are four betting rounds, and in seven-card stud there are five rounds altogether.

Ante

All draw-poker games require an ante, but it is optional and not usually required in stud-poker games. An ante is money placed in the pot by each player *prior* to the deal, and it belongs to the pot. It is used to "sweeten" the pot and to encourage players to stay in the game in order to chase their ante. Generally the total ante is equal to the maximum bet in the game, but this is a rough estimate. For example, if the game is $5-$10, and eight players are in the game, the ante in a private game should be about $1 per player.

The Nevada casinos and the California poker clubs each have rigid antes on their games, some with no relation to the maximum bet.

Betting Limits

Poker can be played for any stakes, from a penny to unlimited amounts. It depends on the game and the players. Generally speaking, however, game limits run in sequence. A betting-limit sequence might be $1-$2; this would be a $1-$2 game. Or it could be $5-$10 or $10-$20. This is not rigid, however, and some games have wide spreads, such as $2-$20. Again, this depends on the players and the rules they wish to set down before the game.

Player's Options

In poker, the player who acts first on the opening round must open the betting with either the minimum or maximum bet, at his option. Thereafter, on that same betting round, each suceeding player has the following options; He may call the bet by betting an equal amount, he may raise the bet by betting a higher amount, or he may not call the bet at all and drop out of play by "folding" his cards, that is, discarding them.

On every subsequent round, the first player to act may either check or make a bet. If he checks, he remains in the game until another player has bet on that round; then, when it is the opening player's turn again, he must call the bet or fold his cards.

He cannot check and then raise. Unless a check-and-raise rule is agreed to beforehand, no player, after first checking, can come back and raise a bet. Check-and-raise is allowed as a right in many casino and poker club games, but is usually not the case in private games.

The Showdown

After all the betting has ended, and there are two or more players in the game, there is the final curtain of poker, the showdown. The player who is called, that is, who made the original bet or the final raise that was called by the other players, shows his cards. For example, if one player bets first, then another raises and the raise is called, the raiser must show his cards. If they are highest ranked, the other players may concede without showing their cards.

If, however, the called player doesn't have best hand, another player will show his cards and claim the pot. The best hand at the showdown wins the pot.

In high-low poker, both high and low hands claim half the pot, and a player having best high and low hand at one time may claim the whole pot if he called high-low.

3. THE BASIC PRINCIPLES OF WINNING POKER

Correct Money Management

The principle of money management is one that too few players understand, much to their regret. Money management can be boiled down to three parts: (a) how much money to take to a game in the form of a bankroll; (b) how much money to lose; (c) how much money to win. We'll study these one at a time.

Bankroll

A player should never play in a game in which his bankroll is inadequate for the stakes involved. When he does, he will find himself playing with what is known as "scared" money. Scared money is money that is insufficient for the game and puts the player at an immediate disadvantage.

With scared money he cannot afford to lose too many pots, he can't afford to play boldly when he has good cards, and he is a target to other discerning players for their raises and reraises and bluffs, for they can readily see that he is out of his element in terms of money.

So in order to play at your best, you must go into any game with the right bankroll. My best suggestion is to play with at least 45 times the minimum allowed bet as your bankroll. In that way you can play for a long time, withstand a run of temporary bad luck, and use your bankroll to your advantage since there will be others in the game with scared money.

If you're in a $5-$10 game, the bankroll should be at least $225. In a $1-$2 game the bankroll should be at least $45, and so forth. This figure may be higher than some experts suggest, and it is much higher than the buy-ins required in casino games, but it will provide you with a comfortable stake and allow you the option of playing at your best, playing boldly and controlling the game.

In addition to this suggested temporary bankroll, if you have digested the principles and strategies outlined in this book, have played a number of games of poker, and feel that you can make a living at it, or in any case augment your present income, you should consider a *total bankroll*, money set aside for poker alone, in order to play it as a business.

Again, the principle of scared money enters into your calculations. You may have a bad session; you may have several bad sessions in a row. Those things happen. In the long run, as a player with more skill and insight than your opponents, you're going to win, but you must always prepare for possible losses.

I would suggest a bankroll of 200 times the maximum bet in the games you're going to be playing in. Thus, in a $5-$10 game you should have $2,000 in reserve. This figure is for those players who want to make a living at the game, not for those who merely want to make some extra money now and then.

The 200-times-maximum-bet figure is about five times the 45-times-minimum-bet temporary figure suggested for an individual game, but it will give a player a substantial reserve, enough to carry him over the worst bad luck or losing sessions.

Finally, we should know where our bankroll is coming from. If we are playing with rent or food money or money that should be paying the children's bills, then no matter what the bankroll consists of, no matter how big it is, it has been turned into worse than "scared" money; it is "desperate" money. Money that is essential for one's survival should not be used for poker. Play only with money you can afford to lose, money that won't mean that much to you if it goes into poker pots and doesn't come out again. If you get into a bind, where your children's next meal depends on your winning a pot, you're a compulsive gambler and shouldn't be playing at all.

Therefore, to prepare for the game correctly in terms of money management, we should provide for a stake of 45 times the minimum bet allowed. If we are going to play the game for a living, we should provide for a stake of 200 times the maximum unit bet as an overall guide. Lastly and most importantly, we should play with money we can afford to lose even though we don't intend to lose it.

How Much Money Should You Lose?

This may sound like a strange question, but it is of utmost importance in preparing for a game of poker. We should always know before we enter any game precisely how much we will allow ourselves to lose.

The next poker game we may be involved in is not going to be the last one on earth. There will be many others, and we want to be able to participate in as many as we can, so we must protect ourselves from being tapped out by one run of bad luck.

We must conserve our bankroll. To do this, we must set a limit on how much we can lose in any one game or session. The limit I suggest is 40 times the minimum bet of the game. If it is a $5-$10 game, then we should lose no more than $200.

What happens when we lose this much? We get up and get out of the game, period. We've had a bad session, the cards haven't been kind to us, we may be in a crooked game, and so on. I can't list all the reasons for losing because several may be beyond our comprehension at the time of the game.

Generally speaking, however, when you lose a great deal of money in any one game, it's not because you haven't been getting good cards. It has been because *you have been getting good cards*, but other players have been getting better cards, thereby beating you out of big pots, pots in which you might have invested quite a bit of your capital.

This can happen for several reasons, and these reasons may be legitimate or otherwise. You don't know. But you get out. You might have had a bad night, you might have been taken by card sharps, or the deck might have been stacked or marked. There may be no way of knowing, but when you've reached the limit of 40 times the minimum bet, get out. By this time you'll be tense and nervous, fatigue will set in, and you'll lose perspective. Get out. Get out when you've lost the limit I suggested, and you're out in time.

If you stay in to recoup, the chances are heavily against that happening. You're on a bad streak, and you don't know the reason for it. You're tired and unhappy, your game is bound to deteriorate, and playing under this kind of stress will only make you a bigger loser.

How Much Should You Win?

Again, this question should be answered in your mind before you sit down to play. You want to leave a winner if possible, and there can be no arguing with one who does. However, leaving too small a winner might be foolish, as foolish as leaving too big a loser. So we work out a formula for winning.

You've come to the game with 45 times the minimum bet. Your goal should be to double the money you brought to the game, in other words, to win 45 times the minimum bet.

This may take quite a while, but if you're winning consistently, if you find yourself getting good cards and having those cards hold up, if you find the competition weak, then you want to stay around and gather up all the cash you can.

So you set that goal. It's generally hard to go beyond it, but of course it's possible. When you reach that point, you can get up and leave, but it's better to stay and play with 20 percent of the winnings; then, if that sum is lost, you must get up and leave the game.

Suppose, in a $5-$10 game, you've won $225. All right. You're a big winner and have reached the outer limits of your expected win. However, the cards are still going your way. You now invest 20 percent of that $225, $45, and if you lose that $45, you're out of the game, no ifs, ands, or buts.

In others words, you're allowing a retreat of no more than 20 percent of your winnings, with the expectation that you will be able to win even more money. If your good fortune continues, stay in the game. If you win another $100, then again use the same principle, continuing to gamble with 20 percent of your total winnings. Keep going until you lose that 20 percent, and then get out.

You may find yourself ahead $800. In that case, you play on till you lose $160 of that money. What happens if you never lose that 20 percent but keep winning? Then keep playing as long as you can keep your eyes open. You're heading for a magnificent win, a beautiful session of poker - take full advantage of it.

This is a "stop-loss" system, the same method used by investors in the stock market, who, after having a stock rise, set loss limits against their profits by automatically selling out at certain prices. This method allows us to let our winnings ride and limits our losses from those winnings.

Studying Your Opponents

In practically all poker games you'll enter, your opponent will not be the casino or card club, like it is in blackjack or craps, but other players like yourself. You'll be paying a house cut or rake, paying by the hour, or, in a home game, playing without any rake or rental.

It is those other players whom you will have to study and understand. If you don't study their behavior, their strengths and their weaknesses, their habits and mannerisms, you will not be utilizing your full skill at poker.

The first thing you should study in any poker game is whether you trust the other players. Is the game on the level? Are other players working in collusion or as partners?

I'm not asking you to be paranoid about the situation, but these questions are definitely to be answered in your mind when you sit down to play.

I recall a game I was invited to in New York City a number of years ago. The friend who invited me was a heavy loser in the game, and within ten minutes of sitting down I knew that something was wrong. Something was definitely off. I couldn't put my finger on it except perhaps to notice that the ordinary rhythm of poker games was missing.

The whole game seemed choreographed. The games moved along at a quiet pace, as though predetermined by someone pulling strings. Cards were shuffled, cut, and dealt, and for all I knew, they had been previously stacked in a certain manner. I felt like I was a participant in those old movies in which the actor playing the farmboy or hayseed sits down with card sharps and is immediately dealt four aces.

I was dealt a full house, kings full, on the second hand in a game of seven-card stud and lost the pot to four deuces. Of course, I had made some big bets and had been raised and reraised not only by the player holding four of a kind but also by two other players, who folded at the showdown. I couldn't figure out what they held from the open cards, but what also impressed me was that of the four deuces in my opponent's hand, only one showed on board. The rest were in his hole cards.

On the next hand I was dealt three wired queens. Well, they sure looked beautiful. An ace opened the betting, a king raised, and now it was my turn. I folded them.

A few eyebrows were raised. I caught these surprised looks because I was looking for them rather than at my cards. I got up and cashed in, called my friend over after the hand was played, which he had lost with an ace-high flush, and told him the game was crooked and to come home with me.

He didn't want to believe me, so I left by myself. I was being taken, no doubt about that. I could just smell cheating in the air.

The next morning my friend called me and said he had lost over a thousand dollars the previous night. I told him my complete feelings about the game, but he still didn't believe me. After all, he worked with two of the guys and had gotten to know the others. They were "great guys." Oh, yes, I told him, great guys, all right, and they'll be your friends till they clean you out.

He took one more bath in that game, then packed it in, still not believing me. Well, maybe I was paranoid, but I doubt it. I have other quirks, but paranoia isn't one of them.

After you ascertain that the other players are honest, you must still study them. The first thing you want to find out is which players are weak and which are strong. Then play accordingly.

A weak player will stay in with cards that only a miracle will help; he will chase hand after hand and be a heavy contributor to the pot.

The tight, strong player will be content to go after those hands he believes he can win. He is, however, easier to push around than a weak player. A strong player will not be ashamed to be bluffed out of a pot; a weak player will.

When you see a tight player, you can assume automatically that he is a strong player. And the bigger the stakes, the more strong players will be in the game.

Also, take advantage of "tells," which are mannerisms players have that give away their hands. When you are out of the game after folding a particular hand, study the players for tells. See which players give away signals when they have either powerful or mediocre hands. Which players are nervous when they have weak hands? How does that nervousness or anxiety reveal itself? Keep alert. Keep examining the opposition.

By the end of a few deals you should have determined which players are strong and which are weak. And you should know which ones give away signals in playing or betting their hands. The more knowledge you have, the better off you'll be. I know for a fact that relaxed people tend to lean back in their chairs. Anxious people lean forward.

A parole-board officer gave a televised interview in which he said that he voted against parole for a convict who leaned forward when answering key questions about his future. He felt the convict's anxiety gave him away, that he wasn't telling the truth.

These are factors to study. Little gestures mean a lot. A former world chess champion adjusted his tie when satisfied with his position. If he didn't adjust his tie when he was in a complicated position, his alert opponent immediately began looking for flaws in the position.

And in poker. When you see a player automatically make a certain gesture when satisfied with his cards, remember that gesture. When he doesn't make it with a big pot at stake, raise him the limit. Of course, it's impossible to enumerate all the tells and giveaways, for they are so personal to individual players, but you should be alert to tells expressed by personal mannerisms, such as shaking hands, a raised voice, a pulse beating in the temple, etc. When you have that information, it's like seeing your opponent's hole cards.

Stay in with Cards That Will Win

I should say, stay in *only* with cards that will or can win the pot at the showdown, to make it perfectly clear. If you do that and that alone, you'll be a winner in poker.

You must have the patience to fold cards that can't win, that might look good but don't have the power to beat a strong hand at the showdown. Study the strategy for each individual game mentioned in this book because this information about what cards to stay in with is of paramount importance.

The easiest way to discipline yourself to do this is to realize that only the top hand wins at the showdown. Second - and third-place hands have no value whatsoever. All the holders of those hands do is feed the pot, and a pot can be a very hungry monster.

It doesn't matter how tight you play, or whether or not you get a reputation as a tight player. You must play with good cards, cards strong enough to win the showdown. If you're in with weaker cards, you're a sucker, period.

Play Percentage Poker

This is very important to remember. If you are going for a flush or straight in draw poker, there should be at least 5 units in the pot for the unit you're going to bet. If they're not there, don't make the bet. The odds will be between 4 1/2 -1 and 5-1 against getting that flush or straight, and you don't want to get 3-1 odds on those bets.

The Money in the Pot is Not Yours

This principle is a difficult one for poker players to understand. When you make a bet, it is no longer your money; it belongs to a common pot. Only the best hand can win that pot and get that money. If you don't have the best hand, how much you have in the pot already won't help you.

The corollary of this is: Don't throw good money after bad. All the money you dump into a pot will be lost if you don't have the top hand or can't drive out the other players. So think of the money in the pot as no longer yours. What you have on the table in front of you is your money.

You need money to bet with. Conserve your capital. Don't get rid of it merely because you already have bet a lot of money into that particular pot. If you can't win the pot, take a deep breath and dump your cards instead of your money.

When You Have the Top Hand, Make the Others Pay

I'm putting this advice last, but it certainly isn't least. The principle of making money at poker depends on getting a lot of money into the pot when you have the top hand. When you have strong hands, you should build up the pots for yourself by betting correctly. If you have the best cards, and others have to buy to beat you, then bet the limit; if raised, reraise the limit.

Make those other players who need to draw or buy cards to beat you pay through the nose for that privilege. Don't let them breathe. Hit them and hit them again with big bets. To be a winner in poker, you need this killer instinct.

When, however, the cards you hold are so strong that you will win no matter what cards they buy, lull them into thinking they have a chance. Call bets instead of raising, check occasionally, but on the last two rounds go all out. By now they may have bought some good cards and feel they have to stay for the showdown. This is the time to punish them with big bets.

Conversely, if you don't have the top hand, get out if the betting gets heavy. Don't hang around and absorb punishment in the hope of buying some random card.

If you follow these six principles, you will win big pots and drop out with relatively little loss when you can't win. You will be able to be a consistent winner in any game you enter and will have a decided advantage over other players. Study these principles well, put them into operation together with the strategies for individual games, and reap the rewards.

4. DRAW POKER, JACKPOTS (JACKS OR BETTER)

Introduction

Draw poker is the closed version of poker and is sometimes called closed poker. The terms "closed" and "draw" both describe this form of poker accurately.

All the cards are dealt closed, so that only the player sees all of his cards. After one betting round there is a "draw," in which any player still in the game may, at his option, discard some cards from his hand and draw new cards, which are also dealt closed.

In jackpots a hand of a pair of jacks or better must be held to open the betting before the draw, thus any higher ranked hand is qualified to open. This is high draw poker, as opposed to the low form of draw poker, known as lowball.

Basics of the Game

Cards

The standard 52-card deck is used, without the jokers.

Object of the Game

To win the pot. This can be done in the two ways discussed earlier. The holder of the best hand at the showdown wins, or if only one player remains in the game because the others have dropped out, the pot belongs to him.

Rank of the Hands

See Chapter 2 - Fundamental Rules of Poker.

Rank of the Cards

The ace is the highest-ranked card, followed by the king, queen, jack, 10, 9, 8, 7, 6, 5, 4, 3, and finally the 2, the lowest-ranked card. The suits have no particular ranking; they are all equal.

Number of Players

Two to 8 can play; the best game is with 6 to 8 players.

Betting Rounds

There are two betting rounds: one before the draw and one after the draw.

Ante

An ante is standard in draw poker. Each player must put in money before the cards are dealt to sweeten the pot. Once in the pot, it cannot be withdrawn and belongs to the pot.

Usually the ante bet by each individual player is much smaller than the minimum bet. For example, the total ante is usually about the maximum bet allowed. If there are eight players in a game, and the betting range is $5-$10, the individual ante would be $1.

There are no standard antes. It is up to the players themselves to agree beforehand on the size of the ante.

Jacks or Better Openers

This game is unique in that a minimum holding is required before a player can open the betting. Therefore, a player opening the betting must show his openers after the game is completed. If he folds, he must put his cards to one side, showing the openers after the game is over. If he has split his openers, he must put the split opener face down to one side, to be shown after completion of the game. This is a strict rule and should be rigidly enforced by the players.

Choosing the Dealer

After all the players are seated, the cards are cut to determine the first dealer: The player cutting the highest-ranked card begins the deal. After this player deals, the deal moves around the table in clockwise order, all the players having an opportunity to deal.

It is a distinct advantage to be the dealer in draw poker since the dealer bets last and draws cards last.

The Deal

After the first dealer has been chosen, he shuffles the cards thoroughly and gives them to the player on his right to be cut. The purpose of cutting cards is to prevent a dealer from stacking the cards in a particular order, but it is a poor safeguard against cheating. If the player to the dealer's right refuses to cut the cards, any other player may do so.

Before the dealer gives out any cards, he makes certain that every player has anted. The purpose of the ante is twofold: It sweetens the pot and also penalizes those players who drop out before the draw since they forfeit their ante to the pot.

The dealer now deals out the cards one at a time, face down, beginning with the player on his left, so that he deals the cards in clockwise sequence. Each player, including the dealer, gets five cards in this way, all face down and all dealt so that no player gets more than one card at a time.

The dealer puts the remaining cards, which form the stock, to one side. Cards drawn after the first betting round will come from this stock.

Dealer's Duties

Since every player has a chance to deal several times in the course of a poker session, he not only has the benefits of betting and acting last but also certain duties.

He must run the game he deals; to do this, he first must make certain that all players have anted. Then, once a bet is made, he must make sure that each player bets in turn, that the bets are correct, and that the correct number of cards are discarded and drawn.

Play of the Game
First Betting Round

The player receiving the first cards, that is, the player to the dealer's left, now has the first opportunity to bet. He is "under the gun," in the poorest position at the table since he must be the first player to act, to show strength by opening or weakness by checking.

In jackpots a player has the option of opening the betting if he holds jacks or better but is not required to open. If a player holds a pair of queens or two small pair, he might not want to open, feeling that these cards are too weak to win at the showdown. So he merely checks, waiting for another player to open. If the entire betting round is checked, the player holding a hand that could have opened cannot now claim to open the pot. Once he has checked, he has forfeited this right. The situation in which either no player is able to or none is willing to open is discussed later in this chapter.

If a player checks before any player has opened, he is not out of the game but can come back and bet by calling the bet. He cannot raise, however, because check-and-raise is not permitted unless all the players agree to it beforehand. If there is no general agreement, check-and-raise is not allowed.

After the bet is opened, any player thereafter must call the bet or raise to stay in the game. If he checks after the betting has commenced, he automatically drops out of the game. This is sometimes called folding, or folding one's cards.

When a player folds, his cards are taken by the dealer and put to one side on a discard pile, separate from the stock, since the dealer doesn't want to give players cards after the draw from cards already dealt to and discarded by other players.

After a bet has been made, players call or raise that bet, and if all bets are correct, the first betting round is over. Those players who have not folded can now draw cards.

The Draw

Suppose there are three players in the game. Each draws cards in consecutive order. To draw cards, a player discards cards face down on the table and asks for the same number he has discarded. In many games of draw only three cards are allowed as a maximum draw by any one player.

If a player drops three cards on the table, he gets three more cards dealt to him. Now the dealer deals all three at one time, from the top of the stock. Another player may want one or two or three cards also and follows the same procedure.

Any player may decide to draw no cards at all and "stand pat" with his hand. A player may stand pat because he has a flush or straight already; to discard any card would weaken his hand.

All discarded cards are placed in the discard pile, out of play. Should there not be enough cards left to draw from the stock, the dealer can then shuffle up the discard pile, have the cards cut, and then deal out drawn cards from that pile.

Although this happens very infrequently, it may happen in a game with eight or nine players in which most have stayed in to the end, drawing many cards. When this situation occurs, the player who is to get cards from the discard pile puts his own discarded cards aside so that he is not dealt the same cards he discarded.

Second Betting Round

After all the players have received new cards, another round of betting ensues. Players can check or bet in this round, but the opener, who goes first now, can check and still remain in the game as can the other remaining players unless another player subsequently bets. In that case, all players who previously checked must call or raise that bet or fold their cards.

After all the bets are made, the player called, that is, the player who bet first and whose bet was called, or who raised last and whose raise was called, shows his cards.

The Showdown

Final hands are shown at the showdown. The player called shows his hand. If it is best, the other players need not show theirs but may concede the pot to him. If another player or several players have better hands, they show their hands, and the highest-ranking hand shown wins the pot.

Showing Openers

After the showdown is completed and the best hand determined, the opener must now show his openers to the other players.

After this is done, the deal is complete, and a new dealer picks up the cards and prepares to shuffle them as the other players, including the dealer, put in their antes.

Games in Which No Player Can or Will Open

Sometimes in jackpots no player can open the betting with a hand rated jacks or better, or a player holding a hand that can open chooses not to do so, and the entire betting round is checked. When this happens, the cards move to a new dealer. Each player antes again, so that the ante accumulates; on this deal, queens or better are now necessary to open.

If no one can open on this round, the deal moves again, and kings or better can open, each player again putting in an additional ante.

Finally, if that round is passed, aces or better can open on the next round. If no one can open, the procedure is varied. The players can go back to jacks or better or descend one step at a time to kings or better, then to queens or better, and finally to jacks or better.

I remember playing a $10-$20 game of draw poker, jackpots, in which three rounds went by with no one being able to open. By this time the game was aces or better, and with 8 players in the game, each anteing $2, the pot held $48 in antes alone.

I was under the gun, the first player to act, and I looked at my cards. I held four queens, the first time I had ever been dealt four of a kind in closed poker before the draw.

I decided to open with $10, hoping to entice some players into the game with me because it is indeed rare that I am dealt such a hand with a lock on the game. But the game was aces or better; to my dismay, no one was going to buck what they thought were aces in my hand, so all the other players folded. I showed them my four queens, and they all admired my hand, but it did me no good.

Draw Poker - A Representative Game

Let's follow a game of draw poker, jackpots, $10 and $20, from beginning to end to understand it more fully. There are six in this game, five players and a dealer. The ante is $2, so there is already $12 in the pot before the first betting round.

First Betting Round. Here are the holdings:

Player	Hand
First:	6 6 10 9 4
Second:	8 7 6 5 Q
Third:	J J A 3 2
Fourth:	5 5 A 3 2
Fifth:	A A Q 9 7
Dealer:	Q 10 7 3 2

The First Player must check since he doesn't hold jacks or better. The Second Player must also check even though he holds a four straight. The Third Player can open, but it is a weak hand, with only a pair of jacks. However, he is also a weak player and opens the betting with $10. The Fourth Player, another weak player, decides to call the bet with his pair of 5s. As will be seen in the section on *strategy*, a player in the middle position should never go in with less than kings in draw poker, jackpots, but these players are weak and don't know this.

The Fifth Player, sensing that the betting has been weak and knowing he's in with a bunch of weak players, raises with his aces by betting $20. This is a good play because aces are strong in draw poker, and he hopes to drive out the weak sisters or make them call his bet with inferior cards.

The Dealer, who's been dealt a bunch of garbage, folds. The First Player also folds, deciding that his 6s aren't strong enough to take a raise, let alone a bet. Again, this is a wise move. Don't chase hands in any form of poker.

The Second Player, who should fold, is in love with his possible straight and decides to call the raise. He puts in $20, a very weak move since his $20 bet will not receive 5-1 in money from the pot, and the odds against improving to a straight are about 5-1. He's another weak player.

The Third Player calls also, whereas he should have folded the jacks and not even opened with them in the first place. But hope springs eternal among bad players. The Fifth Player comes to his senses, feels that his 5s are going nowhere, and folds rather than see a raise. There are three players remaining for the draw. The pot contains $72; $60 in bets and $12 in antes.

The Draw

The Second Player discards his queen and draws one card. The Third Player discards three cards, hanging on to his jacks. The Fifth Player also discards three cards, keeping his aces.

Second Betting Round. Here are the holdings:

Player	Hand
Second:	8 7 6 5 5
Third:	J J 7 7 3
Fifth:	A A 10 10 9

The Third Player, who opened, goes first after the draw. Having improved to two pair, he bets $20. The Fifth Player, who has also improved to two pair, raises by $20. If the Third Player had checked, the Fifth Player might have checked also since he is concerned about the one-card draw of the Second Player. But he decides that his cards make him top man now, and he's going all out, counting on the fact that the Second Player is going for a flush or straight and that the odds against making it are approximately 5-1.

The Second Player, having bought nothing but a headache with the small pair, folds. He could try and bluff by reraising to $60, but he feels he might not be able to fool the Third Player, who never goes out of a hand.

The Third Player, who now realizes he's probably beaten, calls the raise, throwing good money after bad. Like many weak players, he's afraid of being bluffed out of a pot.

Since he called the Fifth Player, who shows his hand, aces up, the Third Player concedes. However, the Third Player shows his jacks which were his openers, to the table.

The Fifth Player wins the pot, the deal moves to the First Player, and the game goes on.

Strategy in Draw Poker, Jackpots (High Draw)

The first and most important thing to remember is that although you may open with a pair of jacks, you shouldn't do so unless you are to the right of the dealer or the dealer himself. If I held jacks, I'd pass the hand and not open in a seven-man game if I were in any of the first five positions. To open or not is an option all players have; merely because they can open doesn't mean they are forced to open.

In the average six-to eight-man game of draw poker, kings or aces as a single pair are the minimum holding you should have to open. If you don't have cards of this strength, get out, because if you open with jacks or queens and are raised, you're in a very bad position. If you call the raise, you can be sure that you're investing additional money on the second-best hand.

The second most important thing to remember is not to stay in with cards that need improvement to win when the odds against improving are more than the odds received for the bet. I'll explain this principle clearly.

Suppose you have a four flush, needing to draw a fifth card of the same suit to make the hand, which is worthless otherwise. A four flush or a four straight has little value by itself, of course. The odds against improving a flush are about 4 1/2 -1. If you bet a dollar, and there are at least five dollars in the pot, your bet is good because you're getting the correct odds. But if you bet a dollar, and the pot contains only three dollars, you are getting 3-1 on a 4 1/2 -1 longshot. You're making a sucker bet.

The simplest way to win at draw poker is to get out when you have weak hands that can't win the pot, or when your bet will not give you the correct odds, for example, when trying for a straight or flush. If you do nothing else, this principle alone can make you a consistent winner.

What cards do you stay in with? If a player has already opened, you must figure him for a pair of jacks or queens. If you have a pair of jacks or queens, get out. You may have a duplicate pair, and your hand is absolutely dead. When another player has opened, I wouldn't stay in with less than kings.

When a player has opened the betting in jackpots, and you hold kings or aces, raise immediately. This serves two purposes: First, you are adding money to a pot that you have a good chance of winning at the showdown, with the hope of getting other players' money in as well. Second, you are forcing the players acting after you to make a decision as to whether or not to see your raise. You will be driving out players who might stay in with a low pair and luckily buy a card to give them three of a kind, such as three 5s, which will beat you. The other side of the coin is that by raising you're forcing weaker players who stay in with poor hands to put more money into the pot in the hope of improving after the draw. Finally, you put the issue right to the opener, and from his betting stance you get a good "read" on his hand.

Let's see how this works in a representative hand. We'll know only our cards, and we'll be the Fourth Player.

The First Player passes. The Second Player opens with a $10 bet. The Third Player calls. You hold AA Q83. You bet $20, raising the opener. The Fifth Player folds, as does the Sixth Player. The Dealer calls the raise.

Now the bet moves around to the opener again. He has several options, including a reraise, but he merely calls your raise with another $10 bet. By doing so, you can now figure that he has a weak pair as openers, either jacks or queens. If he held strong cards, such as three of kind, he'd be in a perfect position to reraise.

Three players remain in for the draw. The opener, you, and the dealer.

The opener draws three cards. You draw three cards. The dealer draws only one card.

You pick up your own cards. You've bought a pair of 4s to go along with your aces and now hold aces up. The opener checks, so you know he hasn't improved to three of a kind. Now your only concern is the dealer.

On the first round he called your raise. If he had two small pairs, he'd have no business remaining in the game, and if he held a four flush or four straight, he'd have been foolish to take a raise and stay in on expectations. You count the pot. There's $84 in, including the ante, and it cost the dealer $20 to stay in, about 3-1 odds on a 4 1/2-1 or 5-1 longshot.

But what did he have? He didn't reraise. He must have gone in with his four flush or weak two pair; otherwise, he had every right to reraise. You must just figure him for a weak player.

Still, even if he is weak, he might have bought that flush or straight. It's not impossible. If we bet now, and he has caught it, we'll be hit with a big raise, and we'll have to decide whether or not he's bluffing.

There's no point in betting now. We've driven out the weak sisters with our raise before the draw. We have the opener beat, and he'll probably fold if we bet. If we bet, and the dealer hasn't bought his flush or straight, he'll also fold. There's just no point in betting. We check.

The dealer also checks, and we all show our cards. We have aces up, the opener shows his queens, and the dealer shows a four flush. We've won the pot without any risk.

This leads to another principles of poker, applicable to all variations of the game. If you have the best hand going in, make the others pay dearly for the right to try and improve their hands because, for the most part, the best hand going in is going to be the winning hand.

Let's study another imaginary deal. This time you're the dealer, in the best position on board. You bet and act last before the draw; thus, you can, with good cards, control the game. In fact, an important rule to follow is this: If you are playing dealer's choice, which means the dealer has his choice of games, always play draw poker. It gives you an immediate advantage because you bet and act last.

After this deal, you again hold aces. The First, Second, Third, and Fourth Players pass. The Fifth Player opens, the Sixth and Seventh Players call, and you raise.

The opening bet was $10, and you raise it to $20. The First, Second, Third, and Fourth Players fold. The opener calls the raise, the Sixth Player folds, and the Seventh Player calls the raise also.

You're still in a perfect position. You'll be the last to draw cards and the last to bet after the draw, so you can study the other players' draws and bets before you have to make any decision.

The opener draws three cards, the Seventh Player draws two cards, and you draw three cards. You can now read the other players' hands as if they were open. The opener is holding jacks, queens, or kings, and nothing else. The Seventh Player drew two cards, but he doesn't have three of a kind; otherwise, he'd have reraised you. You can count on him for a pair and a king or ace kicker. He's a weak player, and you've already made him pay for the privilege of trying to improve his hand.

The opener checks, the Seventh Player checks, and you simply bet the limit, still not looking at your cards.

The opener calls the bet. He can't raise because, unless otherwise agreed upon, there is no raising after a checked bet, and the Seventh Player folds like the weak player that he is.

Since you are called, you show the aces and whatever else you've bought, and you'll win the pot. The opener will probably show you a pair of queens. He was afraid you were bluffing and trying to steal the pot, although his cards couldn't win most pots.

This brings us to another rule. Don't throw good money after bad. Don't be afraid of being bluffed out of a pot if you have mediocre cards. Respect a strong player's big bet. He usually has the goods.

To sum up the strategies of draw poker:

1. If I'm in the first four positions of a 7-man game, I wouldn't open with less than kings. In the fifth position I'd open with queens, after that with jacks.

2. If I opened with jacks or queens and was raised, I'd throw those cards away in a hurry. I'm dead with a weak pair of ladies or knaves, and I don't want to invest any more money in the hand,

3. If another player opens, and I hold kings or aces, I raise.

4. If I hold three of a kind, jacks or better, I call the opener and don't raise. I'm pretty sure it's going to be my pot, and I want as many players in as possible, contributing to my future income. However, should there be a raise after my call, I reraise. Now everyone will have to pay dearly to try and draw better cards than my powerful three of a kind.

5. If I hold three 10s or lower, I raise the opener since any player may draw a third to a face-card pair to beat me. I want them

out, or I want them to pay more money to try and beat me.

6. If I hold two small pair, and I am the dealer or to the dealer's right, and there are no raises before the draw, I'll stay in with them only if there is one other player in with me. I think two small or medium pair are useless in draw poker. The odds against improving them to a full house is 11-1; generally, they won't win by themselves. I'd never open them unless I was the dealer or to the dealer's right.

More Advanced Strategies

1. If I hold two pair, the top pair being jacks or better, I raise the opener so as to drive everyone out before they get a chance to draw. I don't want someone with a pair of 5s getting that third 5; again, if he's trying for triplets with poor cards, he'll have to pay good money for his efforts.

2. If I hold kings or aces, have raised the opener, and he and I are alone for the draw, and if I'm behind him in position, I alter my draw according to his.

If he draws three cards, I draw three. If he draws two, I draw two. I figure him for a pair and a kicker; otherwise, he would have reraised me before the draw. he'll probably check after the draw, figuring me for three of a kind, and when I make a big bet, he'll probably fold.

3. Never go in with three flushes or three straights. They're sucker plays. Don't try to fill in to an inside straight (10 9 - 7 6) since the odds are prohibitive against improving. And don't go in with two small pair if you have to get a full house to win the pot. There will never be enough money in the pot to compensate for the 11-1 odds against improving.

4. Study your opponents in the game. In draw poker it's easy to spot the weak or strong players. Weak players do the following:

a. They go in with four straights and four flushes when there isn't at least 5-1 in the pot.
b. They raise on four flushes and four straights.
c. They go in with three flushes and three straights.
d. They go for inside straights.

e. They go in with a low pair and absorb several raises, then fold after the draw, not having improved their hand.

f. They open with jacks under the gun.

5. Finally, a word about bluffing. You can't bluff a weak player who is winning or about even. You can more easily bluff a strong player, but be careful. A strong player stays in with good cards, and instead of finding yourself bluffing him at the showdown, you might find yourself reraised by a full house or a flush.

Draw Poker, Anything Opens

This is a terrific variation of draw poker, jackpots. In this variation, it's not necessary to hold jacks or better to open the betting. Anything opens.

It's a better game than jackpots and, I believe, more skillful. It's more of an action game because rarely are complete rounds passed. Usually some player is opening.

The same rules apply to anything opens as applies to jackpots, with the one exception that a player in anything opens need not have openers or show openers.

Many players are afraid of this game since they feel it is a "blind" one, but the same principles apply as in jackpots as far as strategy goes. Don't open with less than kings in the first five positions and use the same strategies outlined in jacks or better.

It's an ideal game for a dealer since he can bluff easily if no one has opened, or only one other player has opened.

This game is also played with a "blind bet." The first player to bet, the one under the gun, must bet in the blind, that is, without regard to the value of his holdings. And it's a live blind, which means he can come back with a raise when it's his turn again. This rule makes the pots bigger and makes the game more lively.

Odds And Probabilities in Draw Poker, High

During our discussion of strategy in draw poker we occasionally alluded to the odds against improving certain hands. In this section we'll see how some of those odds are arrived at.

To determine the odds against drawing a straight when we

hold a two-sided straight such as 9 8 7 6 plus an odd card, our calculations are based on the number of cards available to make our straight as against the number of cards that will not make the straight.

Since draw poker is a closed game, we only see our own 5 cards and no others. This leaves 47 unknown cards in a 52-card deck.

In these 47 unknown cards, we know there are four 5s and four 10s. These 8 cards will help us, while 39 other cards will hurt our hand after the draw. Since 39 cards are worthless, and only 8 are valuable, the odds against getting either a 5 or 10 is 39-8, or 4.87-1.

Since the odds are slightly less than 5-1 against us drawing that straight, we shouldn't make a bet unless there is five dollars in the pot for every dollar we bet. If we can't get 5-1 on our money on a 5-1 longshot, we shouldn't make the bet. It would then become a foolish bet.

Suppose we hold an inside straight in which only one card will help us, such as 8 7 6 - 4. What are the odds against buying that 5?

Again, we know only 5 cards, these 4 and the odd card we discard. There are 47 unknown cards to draw to. Of these 47, only 4 (the 5s) will help us, and the rest, 43, will hurt our hand. The correct odds against drawing to an inside straight are thus 43-4 or 10.8-1.

Since draw poker is limited to eight players, and since it is very, very rare for all eight players to be in a pot at one time, there is no way we'll ever get 11-1 for our bet, so if we draw to an inside straight, we're making a pure sucker bet.

The following chart shows the odds against improving various hands:

Cards Held Before Draw	Cards Drawn	Odds Against Improving	
One pair	3	2.5-1	(2 1/2-1)
Two pair	1	10.8-1	(11-1)
Three of a kind	2	8.7-1	(9-1)
Four flush	1	4.2-1	(4 1/2-1)
Two-sided straight	1	4.87-1	(5-1)
Inside or one-sided straight	1	10.8-1	(11-1)

The most important figures to remember from this chart are the odds against drawing to a flush or two-sided straight. If you can't get 5-1 for your bet, don't draw to four flushes and open-sided straights.

The following chart shows the odds against improving various hands after the draw.

Cards Held Before Draw	Cards Drawn	Improving to	Odds Against
One pair	3	Two pair	5-1
		Three of kind	8-1
		Full house	97-1
One pair with ace kicker	2	Aces up	7.5-1
		Any other pair	17-1
		Three of a kind	12-1
Two pair	1	Full house	11-1
Three of a kind	2	Full house	15.5-1
		Four of a kind	22.5-1
Four-card straight flush-open-ended	1	Straight flush	22.5-1
		Any improvement	2-1

Irregularities in Draw Poker
Incorrect Number of Cards

If there are too few or too many cards in the deck, and this is discovered during the playing of a hand, the deal is void, and all moneys bet by the players are returned to them. All previous games played with the same deck stand, however.

No Shuffle

If the cards haven't been shuffled, the game may be declared a misdeal and void any time prior to the second betting round, which is after the draw.

No Cut

If the cards haven't been cut, a misdeal can be declared by any player prior to the first bet.

Exposed Card During Cut, Shuffle, or Deal

There is a misdeal if any card is exposed during either the cut, shuffle, or deal. The cards must be reshuffled again before play resumes. There is only one exception to this rule, and that is if the dealer exposes one of his own cards during the deal. Then the hand stands, and there is no misdeal.

Too Few or too Many Cards Dealt to Any Player

If too few cards have been dealt to any player, and he is lacking just one card, he may be given a card off the top of the deck before the betting has begun. Once betting has begun, the game is a misdeal.

If too many cards are dealt to any player, and he has seen his cards, it's a misdeal. If he notes that he has too many cards before he has looked at the cards and has no more than one too many, he may return the closed card face down to the dealer, who places it on the bottom of the stock, out of play. If a player has more than one too many cards, it is a misdeal.

Skipped Player

If a player is skipped during the deal, it is a misdeal if pointed out before the betting begins. Once the betting has commenced, the deal is firm, and the skipped player stays out of the game.

Wrong Dealer

If the wrong player is dealing, and no betting has been begun, it is a misdeal.

Exposing One's Own Cards Prior to the Draw

If a player exposes his own card, the deal stands since each player is responsible for his own hand's protection.

Betting Incorrectly

Once a bet has been made, it stands, whether done out of turn or in the wrong amount.

If a player bets out of turn, his bet stands, and when it is his proper turn to bet, if his bet is insufficient, he must equal the current bet or forfeit his bet.

If he bets the wrong amount in turn, if it is insufficient, he must make the correct bet or forfeit his bet. If it is too much, it may be considered a raise if the amount is in multiples of bets that are raises in the game. If there has merely been a miscounting of money put in, and it is slightly higher, the excess money may be withdrawn.

An Oral Bet

Any player making an oral bet, such as "I call" or "I see," is bound by the bet and must place his money or chips into the pot.

Any oral declaration, in fact, must be honored, such as "I raise" or "I fold."

Checking Out of Turn

If a player checks out of turn after a bet has been made, he checks out of the game. If there has been no bet, he may still stay in the game.

Exposed Card During the Draw

If a player discovers that he has insufficient cards before the second round of betting has commenced, he may demand and get more cards to fill out his hand. But once betting has begun, he must play with his incorrect hand.

Dealing Too Many Cards After the Draw

If a player has been dealt an excess of cards after the draw and has not put them into his hand or looked at them, the excess card or cards may be taken away by the dealer.

If the player has only one excess card and has placed it in his hand but has not looked at it, the dealer may take away one of the cards drawn by the player.

If the cards have been looked at, the hand is dead, and the player forfeits the pot. If the player doesn't notice the excess card, and at any time prior to the collection of the pot this excess card is discovered, his hand is dead. If the player takes the pot, and only then is the excess discovered, and the funds have been commingled with his own, the hand stands.

Drawing Out of Turn

If a player misses his draw, he may get cards immediately upon noticing the error. If he misses the draw completely through his own negligence, he plays with the cards he has in his hand if betting has begun.

Calling Hands at a Showdown - Mistaken Call

If a player miscalls his hand, giving it a lower value than it has, he is bound by the call if the pot has already been collected by another player and the money has been comingled.

However, if the pot has not been collected, the cards "speak for themselves." If a player miscalls the hand, giving it a higher value, the same rule applies.

Conceding the Pot

Once a player concedes by discarding his hand, he forfeits the pot. However, if he concedes but shows his cards, and his cards are the best hand, the cards "speak for themselves" and supercede his oral concession.

False Openers

If a player doesn't have jacks or better and opens in jackpots, he forfeits the pot even if he has better cards at the showdown. If he opened the betting and wasn't called, he forfeits his bet to the pot.

Insufficient Cards for the Draw

If there aren't enough cards left in the stock to give the last few players or last player any cards to draw, the dealer shall put all the previous discards (but not those of the players yet to draw) together, shuffle them, have them cut by any player but those about to draw, and then deal these cards to the players yet to draw.

5. STUD POKER

Introduction

Stud poker is known as the open version of poker and differs from draw poker in that some of the cards dealt in stud are open cards, seen by all the players in the game. In some variations of stud these open cards may be used as common cards by the participants.

There are many variations of stud, but the player who understands the basic games, which are essentially five-and seven-card stud, will be able to comprehend and play the variations with ease, no matter how wild or complex. With the resources of skill he will bring to the games as a result of his knowledge of the basic games, he'll have no difficulty in mastering any variation.

Five-Card Stud, High

Basics of the Game
Cards

The standard 52-card deck is used, without the jokers.

Object of the Game

The object of all poker games is to win the pot. Again, this can be done in two way. The first is to have the best hand at the showdown. The second way is to drive all the other players out of the game by a playing or betting strategy.

Rank of the Cards

The ace has the highest rank, followed by the king, queen,

jack, and then the cards in order of number of pips on their face; 10, 9, 8, 7, and all the way down to the 2, or deuce, which is the lowest-ranked card. In stud poker, as in all other variations of poker, the suits have no particular ranking and are all equal.

Number of Players

Two to ten players may play; the best game is with six to eight.

Ante

There is usually no ante in stud poker because, unlike draw poker, some of the cards are dealt open, and the game is not as hidden. However, if there are only four or five players, it might be preferable to set an ante so that the pots will be enlarged and there will be more incentive for players to stay in.

Remember that a wise player never chases a bad bet or his ante. The money belongs to the pot, and once it is in the pot, forget about it. Play the cards. If the cards can win, stay in. If not, forget about whatever move you've invested and get out.

Betting Rounds

There are four betting rounds altogether. After the first two cards are dealt, one up and one down, there is the first betting round. Then three more cards are dealt face up, one at a time, and a betting round follows each new card dealt. Eventually all the players staying to the showdown will have five cards, four up and one hidden.

Play of the Game

The Deal

Every player has a turn at dealing in private stud poker games, the deal moving around the table in clockwise fashion. After each deal the deck is passed to the next player, the player on the previous dealer's left, in continuous order.

To select the initial dealer, the players may cut for dealer, and low card deals. The dealer in five-card stud has only obligations and no advantages.

After the dealer shuffles the cards thoroughly, he places the pack face down on the table for the player to his right to cut. After they are cut, he begins the deal. If the player on the right refuses to cut the cards, any other player may cut them.

The deal begins by the dealer giving each player in consecutive clockwise order one card, face down, until all the players, including himself, have this one card. Then he deals another card, face up, in the same order. Thus, before the first betting round, each player has two cards, one hidden and the other face up, seen by all the other players.

After these two cards have been dealt to all the players, the dealer puts the stock aside, and the first betting round commences.

Dealer's Duties

In addition to dealing out the cards, the dealer calls the game. For example, if the First Player was dealt the highest-ranking card, a king, the dealer would say "king bets." He makes certain that the bet is correct, that the betting is in correct order, and that all raises are correct and in proper order. He also collects all cards discarded from dropped hands and puts them out of play on a discard pile.

The Betting Rounds

By the rules of stud poker the player holding the highest-ranking card on the first betting round must make a mandatory bet as an opening bet. If two players have equally ranked cards, the one receiving the card first from the dealer (the player closest to the dealer's left) must make the opening bet.

The game we'll follow has eight players, and the betting range is $1-$2, a small-stakes game. We'll assume that the First Player was dealt the highest-ranking card, a king, and he makes the opening bet. He can bet either one or two dollars, and all subsequent bets and raises may be for one or two dollars. After he bets, the betting round continues in clockwise order, with the player at the left of the opening bettor going next. Each player in turn has the option of calling the bet by betting an equal sum, raising the bet by one or two dollars, or folding his cards and getting out of the game.

Let's follow a typical game round by round to see what happens.

These are the holdings in the first round (* = hidden card)

Player	Hand
First	* K
Second:	* J
Third:	* 2
Fourth:	* 9
Fifth:	* 6
Sixth:	* 10
Seventh:	* 2
Dealer:	* 5

The First Player opens with $1, the Second Player calls the bet, the Third, Fourth, and Fifth Players fold, the Sixth Player calls the bet, the Seventh Player folds, and the Dealer calls the bet.

Since no one raised the First Player's $1 bet, there is now $4 in the pot. The dealer deals out another card, face up, from the stock, again in clockwise order to the remaining players.

Second Round of Betting. Here are the holdings

Player	Hand
First:	* K 4
Second:	* J Q
Sixth:	* 10 3
Dealer:	* 5 A

The highest-ranking open hand now belongs to the Dealer. When we refer to the highest-ranking hand for betting purposes, we always refer to the open cards as seen by all the players. If the closed card were also used for this purpose, it would give away each player's game and make stud poker meaningless.

The Dealer has the option to check or bet. A mandatory bet is only applicable on the first round of betting. If the Dealer now checks, he is still in the game, and when it is his turn again, he may call or fold his cards.

Once a player checks a hand, he cannot then raise. This is known as check-and-raise and is not allowed unless all the players agree beforehand that check-and-raise will be permitted. In the game we're following, it is not permitted.

The Dealer bets $1, and now it is up to the First Player to call, raise, or fold. He calls the bet, the Second Player raises to $2, the Sixth Player folds.

Now it is the Dealer's turn again. He can call the raise, reraise, or fold his hand. He calls the raise by putting another dollar into the pot. The First Player also calls the raise.

Six dollars was bet on this round, making a total of $10 in the pot. The dealer picks up the stock and deals another round of open cards.

Third Round of Betting. Here are the holdings:

Player	Hand
First:	* K 4 4
Second:	* J Q 10
Dealer:	* 5 A Q

The First Player has the highest-ranked hand now, a pair of 4s. He bets $2. The Second Player, who raised on the previous round and holds a possible straight, raises again, to $4. The Dealer calls the raise by putting in $4, and the First Player sees the raise with an additional $2 bet.

Twelve dollars was bet in this round, making a total of $22 in the pot. The dealer picks up the stock and deals the final round of cards.

Fourth and Final Round of Betting. Here are the holdings:

Player	Hand
First:	* K 4 4 7
Second:	* J Q 10 8
Dealer:	* 5 A Q 5

The Dealer is now high, with a pair of 5s showing. We'll peek at his hole card. He's holding the ace, and he never would have gone in unless he could beat the king on board.

On the previous round he should have reraised the Second Player since he definitely held the top hand, and now he's sorry he didn't. He had a perfect spot for doing it.

He wonders if the First Player has three 4s, but then again, the First Player should have reraised on the previous round if he had that strong a holding.

Now he figures the First Player for kings up at the best. The Second Player has been raising continually, but would he have raised with a 9 in the hole, which will now give him a straight? The Dealer doubts it.

The Dealer bets $2. The First Player calls the bet, hoping against hope that the Dealer doesn't have aces or queens up, for he holds a 7 in the hole. If the First Player had been a strong player, when the ace showed in the dealer's hand, he would have folded his cards instead of chasing the ace with his king.

The Second Player raises to $4. The Dealer now reconsiders. Maybe the Second Player does have his straight, but why would he have raised, holding 9 J Q? That's bad poker. But still he might have that straight. The Second Player is a bad player and may have bet in this crazy way and bought his straight. There's only one way to find out.

The Dealer calls the raise, and the First Player folds. The Second Player, called, turns over a jack in the hole sheepishly. He tried to bluff and steal the pot but failed. The dealer wins the pot.

Strategy at Five-Card Stud, High

Five-card stud has become less popular in recent years because of the advent of games such as seven-card stud and six-card stud, both with the variations of high-low. In five-card stud there is only one hole card; thus, the game is relatively open, with little chance for bluffing and hiding the value of one's hand.

Still, five-card stud is a game of skill, and when played strategically, it can be a good money game.

The most important thing to know in five-card stud is what cards to stay in with, and which to fold, at every betting round.

At the outset, before the first betting round commences, you don't want to be in a position to chase hands. You must play a very tight game, going in with the strongest cards possible.

The only cards I'd play are pairs of any kind or a holding with a card that beats other cards on board. That's it, period. If I hold a king, and a player holds an ace, I'm out. If I hold a queen, and another player holds an ace or king, I'm out. And so forth.

After the first betting round, I follow the same principle. If I hold an ace, and another player shows a pair, I don't want to stay in. I have to buy another ace to win, and while I'm doing that, the other player has a chance to improve his pair. So let that be the main strategy in five-card stud, and you won't go wrong. Remember, if you're beaten on board, get out. Don't hesitate, looking at your king in dismay, admiring its strength. It's not worth much against an ace showing.

The best hand to go in with is a pair, back to back, with one hidden. I don't care what pair you have. However, if it is a low pair, below an 8, you're probably going to need improvement to win the pot, if most of the players stay in, so you want as many players out as possible. The fewer players in a game, the better the chances are to not improve and still win.

With 8s to 10s, the middle pairs, you stand a very good chance of winning without improvement, and having a higher pair of face cards or aces, you're almost certain to win with these cards alone. You want to keep the other players in with you.

However, no matter how good your cards, if you see, as cards are bought, that you've become second best, get out of the game. If you have a pair of queens, and another player buys an open pair of kings, you have to retire.

Don't chase superior hands. I can't mention this enough times or state it strongly enough. It's the key to winning money in five-card stud. You must get out with inferior hands no matter how strong these hands are. Three kings are wonderful cards, but you're a poor poker player if you chase three aces with them.

If you play this way, you'll be going out of hand after hand, dropping your cards before the first betting round. You might find five-card stud to be a dull game because of this. But that's the way you're going to have to play the game to win at it.

You may get a reputation as a "tight" player as a result of continually folding your cards, but better to be a tight winner than a loose loser.

The one factor that adds mystery to the game of five-card stud is the hole card, that one unseen card. Five-card stud is a game that's hard to bluff in with only one hidden card because the chances of buying a straight or flush are small with only five cards in hand and no additional buys or draws.

Most hands that will be won will be pairs, two pair, and three of a kind rather than flushes, straights, or full houses. In this way it is a limited game, and a good player can easily tell if his opponent is a weak or strong player after just a few rounds of play.

Once you determine whether or not your opponent is weak or strong, you can start reading his hole card even though it remains hidden. A strong player will not stay in unless he feels he's tops on board. When he shows a deuce, and you have a queen showing, you have to figure him for a king or ace in the hole or a pair of deuces. If you're showing a king, you have to figure him for deuces, or an ace in the hole. He's probably not going to chase a king hand with K 2 since the 2 is very weak.

A weaker player may present more problems, but if you play a tight game, you'll be in only with cards that can beat the weak player on board, and you'll have control of the game more often than not.

When you have the superior hand, you want to make the other players pay heavily for the right to stay in with you. If you hold kings wired, that is, one in the hole and one face up on the first two cards, and players holding inferior cards are willing to call your bet or even raise you, fine. Let them stay in.

On the last two betting rounds sock it to them with maximum raises. Make them now pay for their foolishness. If they're weak enough, they'll pay, for optimism runs rampant among weak players in any poker game.

You must play boldly in five-card stud because there are so few hands that you'll be able to play at all in the course of an evening, and when these come, you want to make the most of them.

So keep these two things in mind, and you won't go wrong. When you're beaten on board, immediately go out. When you're top man, make the others pay to stay in with you. Control the game. It's not hard to do in a game like five-card stud if you have even minimum skills and follow this advice.

Don't go for straights and flushes. They're practically impossible to make. Go for a pair, two pairs, or three of a kind, and count on them to win pots for you.

Seven-Card Stud, High

This is a more popular game than five-card stud for a couple of basic reasons. First, seven cards instead of five are dealt to each player; of the seven the selects the five best to use as his final hand. This gives each player two more cards to choose from and leads to exciting situations, with big hands.

Second, in seven-card stud, there are three hidden cards instead of the one that is dealt in five-card stud. Two closed cards are dealt on the first round, then the last card is also closed. This leads to more betting, bluffing, and bigger pots since those three concealed cards can make almost any kind of hand possible. A player may have four of a kind, with only one card of those four exposed to the other players.

Seven-card stud is a game that many weak players will stay in to the very end, to the showdown, hoping to buy good cards to improve their mediocre hands. It is thus one of the best money games for strong players.

Basics of the Game
Cards
The game is played with the standard 52-card deck, without the jokers.

Object of the Game
To win the pot. This can be done in the usual two ways: either by having the best hand at the showdown or by driving the other players out of the game.

Rank of the Cards
The ace is highest, followed by the king, queen, jack, and then the 10, 9, 8, 7, 6, in descending order down to the 2, which is the

lowest-ranking card in the deck. All of the suits have equal value, none ranking above the others.

Number of Players
Two to eight may play. The best game is played by six to eight players.

Betting Rounds
There are five betting rounds altogether, the first one beginning after three cards are dealt to each player.

Ante
Usually no ante is used in seven-card stud. Antes are required in the casino games and may be used to sweeten the pot if five or fewer players are in the game.

Play of the Game
Choosing the Dealer
Every player deals in turn in seven-card stud. To choose the initial dealer, the cards are cut, and the player with the lowest card is the first dealer. Thereafter, the deal moves in clockwise fashion around the table. There is no advantage to being the dealer in stud poker, and the dealer has several duties to perform.

Dealer's Duties
He must shuffle the cards thoroughly, allow them to be cut, then deal them correctly. He must call the high hand in every round and make certain that the betting is in the proper sequence and that all the players have made correct bets or raises. He is responsible for gathering in all discarded cards and putting them face down to one side, out of play, on a discard pile.

The Deal
After the dealer shuffles the cards thoroughly, he gives them to the player on his right to be cut. If this player refuses to cut them, any other player may cut the cards. Then the dealer squares the pack, putting both parts of the cut cards together, and deals.

He gives one card, face down, to each of the players in the

game, dealing first to the player on his left and so on in consecutive clockwise order, dealing himself the last card, face down. Then he deals another card, face down, in the same manner until all the players, including himself, have two down cards. Then he deals a third card, face up, to each player, including himself, till all the players have three cards, two down and one up.

After this is done, the stock of cards is put aside, and the first round of betting begins. The dealer calls out which player has the highest-ranking card by saying "Ace bets," or, "first ace bets."

To repeat: In seven-card stud there are five betting rounds, and each player who remains to the showdown will receive seven cards, four up and three down.

The Betting Rounds

By the rules of stud poker the player with the highest-ranking card in the first round must open the betting. He cannot check or fold his cards. He may bet the minimum if he wants to, but he must bet.

If two players have identically ranked cards that are highest, the player closest to the dealer's left must open the betting.

After the opening bet is made, all the other players follow that bettor in acting, again in clockwise order. Each player may either call the bet, raise it, or fold his cards, thus dropping out of the game.

Let's now follow a typical 8-man game of seven-card stud, $1 and $2. The * will stand for the unknown cards that are dealt face down.

The following are the holdings prior to the first round of betting:

Player	Hand
First:	* * 8
Second:	* * J
Third:	* * A
Fourth:	* * 5
Fifth:	* * K
Sixth:	* * 8
Seventh:	* * Q
Dealer:	* * 10

Normally, in a game such as five-card stud, the showing of an ace on the first round might drive out most or all of the other players, but here each player has two cards hidden, which may be all kinds of powerful cards, so that the open ace is not that important in seven-card stud.

The Third Player is high man with his ace. He bets $1. The Fourth Player folds, the Fifth Player calls, the Sixth Player folds, the Seventh Player and the Dealer call, the First Player folds, and the Second Player calls.

There are five players remaining left, with $5 in the pot.

Second Round of Betting. Here are the holdings:

Player	Hand
Second	* * J 10
Third:	* * A 2
Fifth:	* * K 9
Seventh:	* * Q Q
Dealer:	* * 10 4

The high man is now the Seventh Player with his pair of queens. He bets $2 on the ladies. The Dealer folds, the Second Player calls, and the Third and Fifth Players also call. There are four players remaining in the game, and the pot contains $13.

Third Round of Betting. Here are the holdings:

Player	Hand
Second:	* * J 10 6
Third:	* * A 2 2
Fifth:	* * K 9 7
Seventh:	* * Q Q J

The Seventh Player is still high. He bets $2 again, seeing little improvement in the other hands. The Second Player folds, but the Third Player raises by $2; the Fifth Player and the Seventh Player call the raise. There are only three players remaining in the game, and the pot contains $25.

Fourth Round of Betting. Here are the holdings:

Player	Hand
Third:	* * A 2 2 3
Fifth:	* * K 9 7 K
Seventh:	* * Q Q J 5

The Fifth Player is high with his pair of kings. He bets $2. The Seventh Player calls the bet, and the Third Player raises by $2. He has been continually raising, and it seems apparent that he has either three 2s or aces up. But the Fifth and Seventh Player call the raise. They are probably hoping to buy a card in the final round that will beat the Third Player's holding. They're chasing his hand, which is not always wise. There is now $37 in the pot.

Fifth and Final Round of Betting. Here are the holdings:

Player	Hand
Third:	* * A 2 2 3 *
Fifth:	* * K 9 7 K *
Seventh:	* * Q Q J 5 *

The Fifth Player is still high, but he checks. Once he checks, he remains in the game, but he cannot raise on this round.

Unlike casino games, check-and-raise is not allowed in private games unless all the players agree to this rule beforehand.

The Seventh Player also checks. Both these checks are telling the Third Player, who seems to be top man, that they haven't bought anything to improve their hands. So he bets $2. Both the

Fifth and Seventh Players call the bet, and the Third Player shows his hand. He has a full house, twos over aces full.

The other players fold without showing, but their hands were definitely losers all the way. Here are the final holdings with all the hole cards open.

Player	Hand
Third:	A 6 A 2 2 3 2
Fifth:	7 Q K 9 7 K 4
Seventh:	A J Q Q J 5 K

A quick critique: The Third Player was the only one who should have gone in with his cards for the opening round of betting. The Seventh Player, with his A Q J holding, had a borderline hand, and when he saw the ace in another hand on board, he had no right staying in. The Fifth Player had an insufficient hand to stay in with. I'd never stay in with less than an A K holding, and preferably if both cards were hidden.

When the Fifth Player saw the queen in the Seventh Player's hand, he should have also folded. Although both the fifth and Seventh Players improved their hands to two pairs, they were in against a strong player who started with better cards in the first place and could have won the pot without drawing or buying another card after his second deuce showed on board.

What this shows is simple, but it is a rule that must be followed if you want to be a winner at seven-card stud. You must go in with only those cards recommended in the section on strategy. Otherwise, even though you'll buy some good cards that will make you a decent hand, you'll be lost from the beginning because the strong players will be in with top cards from the outset and will improve those good cards into powerful winning hands.

Strategy In Seven-Card Stud, High

If you know the correct strategy for this game, you're going to win a lot of money at it. Seven-card stud attracts a lot of weak players who like the action and the fact that they get seven cards, three of which are face down, hidden from the other players.

With five betting rounds, there are many optimists in this game, and most of them, unless they know what they're doing, are doomed to lose because in any poker game, no matter how many cards are unseen or can be drawn to, there is one right way to play the game. Using the correct strategy is going to pay off, especially in such a fast-moving and popular game as seven-card stud, high.

The most important decision any player can make in seven-card stud, the one decision that will determine whether or not he is a loser or winner at this game in the long run, is this: When does he stay in, and when does he fold his cards after he is dealt the first three cards and the first round betting is about to begin?

If you know little else about this game, this alone can make you a winner in seven-card stud. If you stay in with the right cards, you'll emerge a winner. If you stay in with the wrong cards, you'll be whiplashed by raises and reraises, and you'll wind up without the cards necessary to win the pot. The player who stays in with the correct cards finds that the pots he wins are large, and the player who goes in with bad cards will lose the large pots and win an occasional small one.

What I will show is the sound principle of staying in that first betting round with cards that can win, that already have an edge over the other hands. Most players, as I have stated, are optimists and losers. They stay in with the hope of buying some good cards, with the rather dim view of somehow improving their hands so that their cards are contenders at the showdown.

When we stay in with sounds cards and then improve our hands, we are almost sure of having that winning hand at the showdown because we have a definite strategical purpose in mind.

Having written all this, I'll now discuss those hands and only those hands I'd stay in with after the first three cards are dealt.

Cards to Stay in with Before the First Betting Round
Three of a Kind (Triplets)
A holding such as 8 8 8, or any three of a kind, will usually be a winning hand in seven-card stud even if you don't improve them. When you're dealt three of a kind, such as three 8s, the beauty of this hand is that two of the 8s are concealed.

Holding these cards, I wouldn't raise on the first two betting rounds. Let the other players feel you have a high pair in the hole or are going for a low straight. If a player raises in the first round, simply call the raise.

If a player raises on the second round, you now have to use your judgment. I'd still give the impression that I had little and was going for that straight or two pair. On the third round of betting, reraise, and on the fourth and fifth round of betting, raise the limit.

With these cards, you're going for a full house or four of a kind, both formidable hands and likely winners.

If you're dealt a high three of a kind on the first three cards, such as three queens, you want to hold off raising as long as possible to keep all the players in. This hand will most definitely turn out to be a winner, and you want as much money in the pot as possible. It's disconcerting to raise too early, which is what bad players do, and drive out the other players.

How often have I seen weak players raise on the first round, drive all the other players out, and then, with a disgusted expression on their faces, turn over three kings or queens. They've only themselves to blame, and that's why I say that with the correct strategy, you'll build up big pots for yourself and your winning hands.

A High Pair and an Odd Card

By a high pair I mean aces or any face-card pair, though I would prefer to have at least a pair of queens because queens up is generally a winning hand in seven-card stud.

But dealt any high pair and an odd card, you don't want to fold because this hand can lead to bigger and better things, such as three of a kind, two pairs, and possibly a full house.

A Middle Pair and an Odd Card

By middle pair I would classify all cards from 8s to 10s. This hand is not going to be a winning hand without improvement, and so, though I'd stay in, I'd watch the other bettors carefully. If someone holds an exposed king and is betting as if he'd already paired his majesty, I'd fold and get out.

Middle pairs are all right as long as stronger cards don't show on board. Be careful with them because even 10s over a smaller pair probably won't win. I'd stay in with them for the first betting round, and if no improvement occurred after the next card was dealt, I'd quietly fold them.

A Small Pair and a High Card

Let's suppose I was dealt a pair of 5s and a king. My 5s are weak, as far as pairs go, but I would want to stay for at least one betting round, and possibly two, in the hope of pairing the king or improving the small pair.

With this hand, I'd hope the king was concealed and a 5 showed. Now, on the next round, if a 5 or king shows on the table in another player's hand, I know my cards are virtually worthless, and I'm out. I have little enough to go for, and with each of my cards showing in some other player's hand, my chances get more and more remote.

If no king or 5 showed, and on the fourth round I bought a king for kings up, I might be in a position to control the game with a good raise because now I'd have potentially winning cards.

But I will not take raises and reraises to the fourth round in hope of this. If players are raising and reraising, even if nothing much is showing, I can be sure that what they have concealed is stronger than my weak small pair. I don't want to contribute my good money to *their* pot. No way.

Three to a Straight

If I were dealt three consecutive ranked cards of different suits, such as J 10 9, I'd definitely stay in through the first betting round and through the second betting round as well. If, however, on the third betting round, which is the fifth card dealt, I don't have the fourth to that straight, I'm out.

I'm not going to count on buying two consecutive cards to help me on the last two rounds. I wouldn't stay in for the last two rounds unless all I needed to buy was one card for that straight.

In other words, if you don't have four to a straight by the fifth card, get out. As tight as this is, some players in the big money games in Vegas have an even tighter philosophy. If they don't have four to a straight by the fourth card, they fold their cards. However, I think this is being too tight since it will foreclose a lot of straights that might develop.

Again, I'd use my discretion. If someone shows three of a kind on board, your straight is probably going to be worthless, so get out; as good as your chances are of buying to the straight, his chances are even better of getting that full house.

The higher my straight, the happier I am, because I may be bucking another straight since straights and possible straights are easily concealed in seven-card stud. Also, if I hold an ace-or king-high possible straight and pair the ace or king, I have not only the straight working but a potential two pair headed by kings and aces, which is a winning hand by itself.

Three to a Flush

Let's say I'm dealt ♦ J ♦ 10 ♦ 5. I hold a three flush. I'd use the same principle as if it were a three straight, and that is, if my hand doesn't improve to a four flush by the fifth card, then I'm out. Never try to buy two cards you need on the last two rounds. That is a sucker's play, and it will make you a sure loser.

If you're playing against strong players, and they see that you're a player who goes for those flushes and straights against enormous odds, they'll raise you till you're dizzy because they know you have to buy to beat them, and they'll make you pay very dearly for that privilege.

And never, never raise on a possible flush or straight. You're throwing money to the wind because the odds are against your buying it, and why raise when the odds are against you?

Raise when the odds are in your favor. Get your money down then, not the other way around, and you'll be a smart player and a big winner.

Ace, King, and Odd Card

Even though I have no pairs, I would stay in for a round to see what develops because I have two big cards that can be paired and that can lead to a winning hand. I'd prefer to have both cards concealed to play this hand.

These cards can't withstand raises on the first betting round since I assume I'm being raised by players who already have a pair, while I first have to hope to pair the king or ace and then get another pair to win. In other words, I'm supercautious going in with these cards.

A Small Pair, Concealed

Finally, I'd stay in with a small pair that's concealed, but I'd prefer my odd card to be a queen or higher. With a face card and a small concealed pair, I'd stay in for two betting rounds unless my cards were showing on board.

If I hold a small concealed pair accompanied by a middle or low odd card, I'd stay in only for the round. And if my pair is not concealed, I may just drop them anytime the betting gets rough, even on the first round.

I have little confidence in a small pair because unless they turn into three of a kind, I have no real chance of winning that showdown, 8s over 3s are not going to win, and so if I don't have a high card, such as queen, king, or ace, to shield the small pair, I'm out.

Many players will stay in with a small pair to the very end because they feel guilty about dropping out of a game holding a pair. I don't let guilt enter into the picture, and neither should you. The only consideration is, Can my first three cards develop into a winning hand, the best hand on the table? If not, throw them away. Occasionally, you'll regret the decision, but in the long run, and we have to think if the long run in talking about skill and strategy, you'll be doing the right thing.

Other Strategy in Seven-Card Stud

I've devoted a lot of time and space to the cards that I'd stay in with because I feel that that's the most important aspect of the strategy.

Since we're only going in with good cards, we'll be considered tight players by those losers who feel it is their duty to go in hand after losing hand. So we must vary our opening strategy at times. On rare occasions we'll go in with junk just to keep the other players alert. However, once we're raised, we must fold the bad hands.

Betting and Raising

When my cards are very strong, strong enough by themselves to win without any improvement, such as three of a kind in face cards, I want everyone in the pot; so I disguise my strength by not raising immediately. If there are a couple of raises in the early rounds, I'll just call them until the opportune moment, which is the last two rounds of betting. Then suddenly, my hand will assert itself in raises.

I can remember a particular hand vividly because it was in a big game, against a bunch of stringers who pegged me as a weak player. I was dealt Q Q 8. I stayed in, of course, and there were no raises on the first round of betting.

Then I bought another queen, and my hand read Q Q 8 Q, with two of the queens concealed as hole cards. One player had a pair of jacks showing, and another player showed a pair of kings. The fourth player had two spades showing.

The kings bet, the jacks raised, and the spades and I called the raise. The kings weren't too strong because already one king had showed among the hands that folded.

On the next round I was dealt a 9, so my hand showed Q Q 8 Q 9. The kings were still high on board and checked, the jacks bet the limit, the two spades, which had become three spades headed by an ace, called, as did I. The kings folded.

On the sixth card I paired the 8s and now held Q Q 8 Q 9 8. Not having raised till now, it was hard for the other players to figure out what I had. I might have been holding aces in the hole, or an 8, or I was going for a high or medium straight.

The jacks were now high, his hand showing J J 10 5, and he bet the limit. The three spades were still three spades, but on the last card he had bought a queen of hearts, the "case" queen (case meaning the last, or fourth, card of any particular rank).

The spades called the bet, and I raised the pot. Now both players took a good look at my cards. I figured the jacks for three of a kind, and I had the feeling that the spades were already an ace-high flush, and he had been playing possum, along with me.

But they now had to gauge my hand. The pair of 8s looked like it might be three 8s because no other 8s were showing. Or perhaps I had queens up. The jacks went up one more time, the spades called, and I called.

I only called because I was hoping to suck the jacks in on the last round, when he might buy a full house. If he already had a full house, even better.

On the last card I bought another odd card since there was nothing I could buy to improve my hand. The jacks were still high, and he counted the pot and bet it. He had bought his full house.

The spades were now in the middle, and after a long bout of uncertainty, he dropped out. I reraised the pot. The jacks looked me over, figuring that I had not more than three 8s full. The holder of the jacks had beaten me out of a couple of pots earlier when I didn't show my cards, and he figured I was a weak player because my open cards had previously indicated that I was raising on possible flushes, whereas I had three of a kind, unfortunately inferior in rank to his.

After a long pause, he reraised the pot, and I had to put in all my money just to call since the game was table stakes. If I lost, I was tapped out. A bit of anxiety came over me, wondering if he had four jacks, and if he did, good luck to him. But all my feelings were directed to the fact that he held jacks full, had pegged me for 8s full, having seen a queen drop on the last card in the spade hand.

Sure enough, that's what he had, jacks full. I showed my queens full, saw his angry face, and inwardly felt good. He had been showing his colors from the beginning, while I stayed back, laid back as it were, until I hit with my big guns.

I won a lot of money on that hand, over a thousand, and that's why I remember it so well. And I had played my cards carefully to squeeze out the maximum amount from the other players.

If I hold strong cards, but not overwhelmingly powerful cards such as kings or aces up, I raise as soon as I can. I want to drive out the players who are going after triplets or a flush or straight. I figure that I'm top man at the moment, and If I eliminate the competition, I'll be left alone to gather in the pot.

At this point, with my aces or kings up, I want to weed out the remaining players so that, at the showdown, I only have to face one other player, if possible. I don't want four players stringing along with me to the showdown, any one of whom might get lucky and improve a low pair to triplets or buy that flush on the last card.

If I hold kings or aces up, and a player is going for a straight or flush, I keep raising and betting big to make him pay heavily for the privilege of buying cards.

Again, I repeat this strategy because it's very important. When you have the top cards, make the others pay heavily for the privilege of buying their cards, for their expectations. Don't be afraid to plunge then; that's the time to do it, to show what courage you have. You can't play scared when you're top man, or else you'll end up a loser in poker.

If I'm going for the flush or straight, I want to go that route as easily as possible. If there are raises, and I feel a player already has three of a kind, I fold fast. I'll be doomed because he can improve his cards to a full house as easily as I can improve to a flush, and I stand no chance.

I prefer a four flush or four straight with an ace or king heading the group, and even better, with a high pair attached, such as K K Q J 10. The kings might be the dominant high pair if I pair up any of the other cards.

To sum up, if you have the best cards, and they will win without any improvement, keep all the players along for the ride, then hit them in the last two betting rounds.

If your cards are strongest, but others might, if allowed to stay in cheaply, luckily buy some random card to beat you, make them pay as heavily as possible for their troubles. In the long run they won't win many of their hands; they'll get their flush or straight once in five or six hands, and the other times they'll be paying you a lot of money.

Never raise on four flushes or four straights. Don't raise on expectations, period.

One final word. Second best doesn't win at stud poker or any other form of poker. No matter how lovely your cards look, no matter how strong they feel in your sweaty hands, don't be foolish. If you're beaten on board, get out.

Don't feel guilty about it, don't feel you have any obligation to your cards. Your only obligation is to yourself, so put pride aside and dump cards that can't win, no matter how great they look.

Irregularities in Stud Poker

The following irregularities have the same rules as in draw poker: incorrect number of cards in deck; no cut; exposed card during cut, shuffle, or deal.

No Shuffle

If the deck hasn't been shuffled, the game is a misdeal if discovered before the first bet is made.

Dealing Too Many Cards to One Player

If a player has too many hole cards but hasn't seen them, nor has the betting begun, the dealer may remove one of the cards at his discretion and place it at the bottom of the stock, sight unseen.

If the player has seen his hole cards, his hand is dead, and he forfeits any bet he may have made. If he doesn't discover that he has too many cards until after the pot is collected, the player can keep the pot if the funds are comingled.

Dealing Too Few Cards to One Player

If a player has too few cards and is short only one card, he may get an additional card from the dealer. If the betting has commenced, or he has more than one card missing from his hand, his hand is dead, and he is out of the game.

Dealing Too Many Hands

Should the dealer have dealt one or more hands in excess of players, and this fact is discovered while only the hole cards have been dealt, then the extra cards should be taken back by the dealer and placed unseen at the bottom of the stock.

Should the extra hand contain an exposed card, that card is shown to all the players and with the hole card placed at the bottom of the stock.

If a player inadvertently takes the extra hand as his own and looks at the hole card or cards, he then plays that hand as his own, and the other excess hand is placed on the bottom of the stock, sight unseen.

Dealing Too Few Hands

If the dealer has dealt one fewer hand than there are players, and this is noted before any of the players have seen their hole cards and before any players have received a card face up, then the dealer may take and use the top card from the stock, dealing it to the player who was left out.

If a card has been dealt face up, or the dealer must give a player more than one card at a time, it is a misdeal.

Skipping a Player During the Deal

If the dealer skips one of the players during the deal, and that card is dealt face up, the card is moved to its correct place, and the deal continues.

Exposing a Card to be Dealt on the Next Round

If a card is exposed by the dealer, and that card is to be dealt for the next round but is known before that round is dealt, the card is discarded and placed on the bottom of the stock.

Exposing Final Closed Card in Seven-Card Stud

If a player receives his final card exposed by the dealer in seven-card stud, he is at a disadvantage, therefore, no raises are permitted on this final round.

Exposing One's Own Hole Card

If a player exposes his own hole card, there is no misdeal since each player is responsible for the security of his own cards.

Betting Out of Turn

If a player bets out of turn, that bet stands, and he cannot change or withdraw it. When it is his proper turn to bet, that bet stands as if it were equal to another player's bet. He cannot now raise. If his bet is not sufficient, it must be increased to equal the other player's bet made in turn. If he doesn't want to equal it, he is considered to have folded his cards. If the previous bet was less than his original bet, his out-of-turn bet is considered a raise.

Oral Bets

Any player announcing an oral bet will be bound by that bet. An oral bet made out of turn is treated as a regular bet made out of turn.

Dropping Out, Out of Turn

Once a player folds his cards out of turn, he is bound by his decision and cannot change his mind and stay in. His hand is dead as of the announcement or the motion of folding his cards.

Dealer's Mistake in Calling

If a dealer mistakenly calls one hand as highest for betting purposes, and that hand opens the betting in any round, any other player may point out this mistake. Then the bet is returned, and the correct hand bets first.

If the dealer or any player calls out the wrong hand as the winning hand, the cards "speak for themselves." Winning cards, based on rank of hands, win the pots, not incorrect calls of winning hands.

However, should the wrong hand win, and the money has already been mingled by the player with his own funds, that win stands.

Mistaken Concession at Showdown

Should a player mistakenly concede his hand after he has called the previous bet but before the pot is taken in by the player to whom he concedes, and if his cards are best, the cards again "speak for themselves," and the conceder wins the pot.

But should he have already discarded his hand, and the pot was mingled with the other player's funds, then the conceder's hand is dead, and he cannot claim the pot.

6. LOWBALL POKER

Introduction

Lowball, or loball, as it is sometimes called, played as draw poker, is an intriguing game sometimes found in the California poker clubs and Nevada casinos. The stud variations are also popular, especially seven-card stud, lowball, known as razz.

Lowball is high poker reversed. All the games we've discussed till now - draw and five- and seven-card stud - are games in which the highest-ranking hand wins the pot. In lowball the lowest-ranked hand wins.

Everything else is the same, with one important exception. Flushes and straights don't count in lowball; they are eliminated from consideration. Thus, a hand reading 8 7 6 5 4 in lowball would be considered an 8 7 high hand. The straight doesn't matter. The same thing would be true if this hand were all of one suit. It wouldn't be a straight flush, merely an 8 7 high hand. The hands are described by the high cards; it is the lowest of the high cards that win, not the lowest of the low cards.

In lowball the ace is always the lowest card, equivalent to a 1. A hand holding 9 6 4 3 A would be read as a 9 6 high hand, the ace reading as 1.

Basics of the Game
Cards

The game is played with the standard 52-card deck, without the jokers. California poker clubs use the joker, and its use there as a semiwild card will be discussed in Chapter 10 "California Club Poker."

Object of the Game

To win the pot. This can be done in two ways: by holding the lowest-ranked hand or by forcing all the other players out of the game by a betting or playing strategy.

Rank of the Cards

The ace is best, followed by the 2, 3, 4, 5, 6, etc., up to the king. The worst cards to hold are the face cards. It is the exact opposite ranking of high poker.

Number of Players

We'll discuss this in each of the variations of lowball.

Ranking of the Hands in Lowball

In lowball the highest-ranking card determines the call of the hand when all five cards are odd cards. A queen-high hand loses to a jack-high hand. For example, Q 8 7 6 2 loses to J 10 9 5 4. A 7-high hand loses to a 6-high hand. Going one step further, a 9 8 hand loses to a 9 7 hand.

To summarize, to determine the winner of the pot, we take into consideration the high card of a five odd-card holding. Whichever hand holds the lower-ranked high card wins the pot.

If both players have identically high ranked cards, the next highest card in their hands is taken into consideration. Whichever hand then has the lowest-ranking second card wins the pot.

If both the highest and second-highest cards are still equal in rank, then the third-highest card determines the winner, and if all these are identical, the fourth, and then the fifth card determines the winner.

If all five cards are of equal rank, the pot is split.

It is usual, in lowball, to call out the hand by mentioning the first two highest-ranking cards. A holding of 10 8 7 4 2 would be called "10 8 high" or simply "10 8."

Here are the ranking hands, starting with the best hand.

5 4 3 2 A. Since straights don't count in lowball, no hand can be better than this one. It is called a "wheel" or "bicycle". When a player puts down his wheel, the pot is his unless another player also has one, which is very, very rare indeed. In lowball, as in other

forms of poker, suits have no relative value, and if two players have wheels, they split the pot.

6 4 3 2 A. The second-best hand.
6 5 3 2 A. The third-best hand.
6 5 4 2 A. The fourth best hand.

It is not important to memorize the relative rankings of hands since by examining the two highest-ranking cards, a winner is usually determined. And if necessary, the other cards in the hand are then taken into consideration to determine best hand. A holding of 8 6 5 3 2 beats 8 6 5 4 2.

The highest unmatched hand is K Q J 10 9. These are terrible cards to hold in lowball, but it beats any pair.

Thus, we see that unmatched cards, that is, five odd cards, are best to hold in lowball. They take precedence over all other hands.

Next in rankings come the pairs. The lower the pair, the stronger the hand. A pair of 2s, for example, beats a pair of 3s. If both players have identical pairs, then the hand is examined to see which highest-ranked odd card is lowest of the remaining cards.

To explain more simply, 4 4 J 9 5 beats 4 4 Q 3 2. The odd cards read J 9 in the winning hand and beat the Q 3 holding. Another example: 9 9 6 5 4 beats 9 9 7 2 A.

We could go on with the relative rankings of hands, but it would be fruitless since they rarely come up in practical situations beyond a pair. No player in his right mind is going to hold three of a kind in lowball, hoping that he'll beat out a full house.

Lowball, Draw Poker

This game is played exactly as regular high draw poker except, for obvious reasons, there is no such game as jackpots, or jacks or better. The game is played as anything opens. The same rules that apply to draw poker apply to this game except that straights and flushes don't count.

Number of Players

Two to nine can play, although seven or eight make up the best game. Very few cards are drawn in lowball draw poker in comparison to high draw poker because there is danger, when drawing several cards, of getting a random high card that will wreck your hand or pairing odd cards in your hand.

Let's study a sample game of lowball draw. As in high draw poker, the dealer has an advantage in calling and acting and betting last. (See the rules of high draw poker for the dealer's duties, the order of dealing and playing, etc.)

A Sample Game. There are eight players in our game. The betting is $3 and $5, which means that before the draw bets and raises are in the $3 limit, while after the draw bets and raises are in the $5 limit. The ante is 50¢.

Here are the holdings before the draw and the first round of betting.

Player	Hand
First:	K J J 9 6
Second:	7 7 6 4 A
Third:	10 8 6 4 2
Fourth:	Q 9 7 3 A
Fifth:	Q Q 10 8 5
Sixth:	J 7 5 4 2
Seventh:	K Q 9 8 8
Dealer:	9 6 5 5 4

There is no blind bet in this game. The First Player may check, and he does. The Second player opens with a $3 bet. The Third Player, with a pat hand, gives it a try by calling the bet. The Fourth Player calls, figuring to unload his queen and try to draw a low card. The Fifth Player folds; the Sixth Player calls.

The Seventh Player folds, the Dealer calls, and the First Player folds.

Here are the holdings of the players now remaining in the game.

Player	Hand
Second:	7 7 6 4 A
Third:	10 8 6 4 2
Fourth:	Q 9 7 3 A
Sixth:	J 7 5 4 2
Dealer:	9 6 5 5 4

Five players remain in the game, and the pot totals $19, of which $15 was bet and $4 was the ante. At this point we can see that only the Second Player and the Sixth Player have any chance at all. The Third Player, with his pat 10-high hand, might have made a bet if he were the dealer and everyone had checked before him, but his hand is practically worthless in this eight-man game.

The Fourth Player and the Dealer are in, hoping to play out the game with 9-high hands. I would never draw to more than a 7-high hand in lowball. We thus see in this game what is generally seen in poker games, a group of weak players competing against a couple of strong players.

All the players, with the exception of the Third Player, draw one card. After the draw, the holdings are as follows:

Player	Hand	Draw
Second:	10 7 6 4 A	(drawing the 10)
Third	10 8 6 4 2	(standing Pat)
Fourth:	K 9 7 3 A	(drawing the King)
Sixth:	7 5 4 3 2	(drawing the 3)
Dealer:	9 6 5 4 3	(drawing the 3)

The Second Player now opens the betting. He's a fairly strong player and knows that his 10-high hand is worthless, so he checks. The Third Player wants to see what is going to happen, so he checks also. The Fourth Player checks, preparing to fold his garbage hand. He threw away a queen and bought a king. No matter what he bought, he couldn't win this game. When players go in with bad cards, they get nowhere, and we see that he's drawn to a possible nothing.

The Sixth Player has a moderately strong hand, a 7 5 holding, made even stronger by the fact that all the players before him have checked. He bets $5. The Dealer, who thinks that a 9 6 hand has value since he is a weak player who stays in with worse cards, calls.

The Second Player folds, knowing now, after two bets, that his 10-high hand is for the birds. But the Third Player calls, afraid of being bluffed out with his pat hand, which he should have discarded in the first place.

Now the showdown. The Sixth Player, who is called, shows his 7 5 high; all the other players moan, and the Sixth Player takes the pot.

Having seen many mistakes made by weak players, we'll discuss the correct strategy for lowball draw poker in the next section.

Strategy In Draw Poker, Lowball

Again, as in so many variations of poker, the most important aspect of our winning strategy is knowing what cards to stay in with before the first betting round begins.

In draw poker, lowball there are two fixed rules we must follow. First, we never draw more than one card. *Never.* The only possible exception to this rule is when the first bettor, no matter what he holds, must bet blind. In that one case, and only then, we draw more than one card if no one has raised our blind bet on the opening round of betting. But if we are not the blind bettor, we never draw more than one card, *never.*

Second, if we draw one card, the highest of our four odd cards should be the 7. Don't go in with four odd cards headed by an 8. It's just too high and will lose more often than not; 7 is our top card when we have to draw one card.

If we know nothing except these two rules, we're on our way to becoming a winner at draw poker, lowball.

That's our basic strategy for holding cards. If we can, we should stay in only with pat hands, and pat hands of 8 or under. If we have a 9 pat hand or a 10 pat hand, they're bound to lose, and we must be careful.

I'll stay in with a 9 pat hand if I'm playing with weak players who are always drawing one or more cards and I'm the dealer or to the dealer's right, and then only if one other player is in with me.

If I stay in with another player with my 9-high pat hand, I still remain cautious. If he stands pat, I may already be beaten, but he may have a high pat hand. So if he checks after the draw, I check. If he bets small, I'll call.

However, if he draws one card and then checks, I'll bet the limit. Let him wonder about that.

Holding a pat hand in this situation also leads to bluffing possibilities. I was in a fair-sized game when I played tightly, as usual, and consistently drew only one card or stood pat. I was a big winner late at night.

In a game I was dealing, the first player bet, another player called, and all the others folded. I looked at my cards. I held a pat hand, headed by a 9. I raised the limit, and they both folded fast.

I could have raised on anything in that position, for I was last in calling and had all the advantages. However, if either called the raise, I wanted to say, "I stand pat," with great assurance, and my raise took care of that. If one player stayed with me, drew a card, and checked, I was prepared to bet the limit. If he had bet, I'd raise the limit. I might have lost, but it would be his heart pounding, not mine.

That's the key to winning poker. Play a tight game, and get control of the game. If you play this way, you will win in the long run. And once you're ahead and playing with good cards, the other players are going to fear you and get scared when you make big bets or big raises. You have them by the short hairs at this point.

Another important consideration is position. If you are dealing or to the right of the dealer, you are in an ideal position to raise or open with cards you couldn't play with if you were under the gun or in the first three positions to bet.

Take advantage of your position. Suppose you hold 7 4 3 2 A. Fine, fine cards. If you're under the gun, you can open these cards with a medium-sized bet, hoping to keep the other players in. However, if you're at the dealer's right, and a few players are already in the pot, you can hit them with a big, big raise.

If they call, you stand pat, and then let them worry. Now you leisurely watch what they draw since you're last to draw, and after the draw you're last to bet.

After a couple of good bluffs before this hand this might be the time the weakies in the game are going to test you to make certain they're not going to be bluffed again. If they open the betting, and you raise and they reraise, you can give them another raise. Unless they have a 6 or below holding, which is an infrequent holding, they're in deep trouble.

Taking advantage of position and staying in only with cards that can win at the showdown will almost guarantee you a winning session of poker.

As you read this, you may ask (by this time being fairly knowledgeable about smart poker) who draws more than one card in lowball? Who? Plenty of players do. Get in a game in any Nevada casino and watch the fools go to work discarding their money along with their cards. You'll be amazed, but don't just sit there with your mouth open. Put your skill to work, and take advantage of their poor play.

Five-Card Draw, Lowball - A Poker Story

Five-card draw, lowball is one of my favorite casino games, and I will always harbor fond memories of a particular game I played in one of the downtown Las Vegas casinos.

The year was 1972, and the month was September, the beginning of September, during the Labor Day weekend. I had just packed up my things and moved from San Francisco to Las Vegas. I was working on a novel at that time that I couldn't complete in San Francisco because the man who lived underneath me was annoyed at my typing, and he continually banged on the ceiling or complained about my work to the manager.

I never typed before nine in the morning or after nine at night, but this neurotic never left his room; after a while, everytime I sat down to write, I tensed up, waiting for his pounding or the manager's knock on the door. Under those circumstances it was impossible to work.

At this time I received an invitation from the president of a Strip hotel with whom I had been in correspondence, inviting me to spend as much time as I wanted to see the inside workings of a casino operation. Eventually, this visit led to another novel, a serious novel about Las Vegas, but at the time, I decided, since August was coming to an end, since I was unhappy in my apartment, and since there was nothing really holding me in San Francisco, lovely as it was, that it was time to get out and try a new place in the West.

I had been in San Francisco for only two months, having moved from the East that June, and so all these cities were new to me. I packed my things, put them into my car, and drove directly to Las Vegas.

Saturday afternoon, in the midst of the Labor Day weekend, I found myself in Baker, California, still 92 miles from Las Vegas. I stopped for gas in that small nondescript town, which is really nothing more than a collection of gas stations, cheap restaurants, and motels, and asked what my chances were of getting a room that night in Las Vegas. The guy pumping gas shook his head; he was a grizzled man in his sixties.

"No way you're getting a room this weekend," he said. "I'd advise you to stay here for the night and then try tomorrow or Monday."

But the thought of staying in Baker was too much even for me, tired as I was. The sun was descending in the west, but the heat was still fierce, and a wind was blowing off the desert, and fine sand blew into my face. All I could see doing in Baker was leaving my dust behind, so I paid for the gas, hopped into the car, and drove on, heading for the mountain passes that finally terminated in the long, graceful drive down into Nevada at Stateline, and then 41 miles farther into Las Vegas.

The whole trip from San Francisco to Las Vegas is 575 miles of tiring, boring driving. I got into Las Vegas at a little after seven in the evening, with the sun already starting to set behind the western mountains of this desert city.

Once in Vegas, I stopped at a Strip hotel, found that I could make free calls to local motels from a house phone, and called about fifteen motels at random. No rooms available.

I inquired at the reservations desk of the hotel I was calling from and found the same answer. I was tempted to call the president of the Strip hotel to which I had been invited to view his operation, but I didn't want to start my stay by asking for favors, and I figured that with all the hotels and motels in this town, there must be something.

I headed downtown. I parked in an open lot run by one of the downtown hotels, worried about all my goods in the car, exposed the way they were, but what could I do? I went into one of the downtown hotels, found that there were no free house phones for local calls, and cashed in $2, getting twenty dimes. I used them up and another dollar's worth before I gave up. No motel or hotel had any rooms available.

Someone who overheard my conversation on the phone told me to try North Las Vegas, which was just a couple of miles away. I went back to my car, drove out of Vegas along Las Vegas Boulevard North, and spent a painstaking hour and a half investigating North Las Vegas, which seemed to me that night like a huge slum area. A couple of flophouses had rooms available that night; one, the Mintz hotel, without even bothering to change the sheets, charged $24 for a room without a bath. There was no way I was going to pay that money to stay in that place.

Two motels were willing to charge me a package rate of $70 for Saturday and Sunday night's lodging in decrepit rooms. I had enough of North Las Vegas. Now really tired, I drove back to the same parking lot, parked the car under bright lights to ward off potential thieves, and went back into the hotel.

It was now almost nine-thirty in the evening, and I could hardly keep my eyes open. I decided that fresh air would be helpful, and I walked out along Fremont Street, which was crowded with tourists.

I found a place that served a 49¢ breakfast at all hours, and I sat and had one, drinking a few cups of coffee to keep my eyes open. After that, I felt a little better and bought a local paper. There were rooms advertised in private houses, and I went back and called their numbers. Some didn't answer, and the others were booked solid. I had definitely come into town on the wrong weekend.

Well, there was nothing for me to do but somehow kill the

night. I went to a casino coffee shop and had another two coffees; then I sat in the keno lounge, hardly able to open my eyes. I had been on the road driving for more than 10 hours, and now my energy was at its low point. Slowly my eyes closed, and I heard vague sounds of numbers being read off in the keno game. I opened my eyes when I felt my shoulder shook. It was a security guard.

"No sleeping here, buddy, he said.

"O.K. I'll keep my eyes open."

"You better move on."

I got up wearily and looked around. The casino was packed with tourists. All the tables were jammed. I decided to try the adjoining casino. I went in, but the same situation presented itself there. I didn't know what to do. I was too tired to read; so I went into the men's room to wash up. My eyes were bloodshot, my face looked pale and unhealthy in the harsh light, and my whole body was perspiring. What I wouldn't have given for a hot shower and a bed to stretch out on.

I washed my face and hands carefully and left the washroom. I decided to find a way to kill time, maybe play a low-limit blackjack game. I knew the game pretty well and felt I could beat the house, but all the tables were packed. A couple of the $5 tables had one spot open, but even those tables were filled with five and six players. I would lose all my edge over the casino with that many at a table. I didn't want to throw my money away. I had only a few hundred dollars in cash and traveler's checks with me, and I'd need most of it as a deposit on an apartment. The rest of my money was in bankbooks, which I'd have to transfer later that week.

I decided to make some more calls. Perhaps I missed a couple of motels that had openings. As I walked to the rear of the casino, I passed the poker pit, and a man asked if I'd like to play some poker. He was a house employee, a fat man in a rumpled white shirt.

"We have a seat open at lowball draw," he said.

"O.K.," I said immediately, happy to be seated. I took the remaining seat in the game, facing 7 other players and a house dealer. The sign on top of the table, suspended from the ceiling, read: "Five-Card Lowball, Draw, $3 and $5, 25¢ ante, $20 Buy-In".

As I studied the sign, the dealer, who was in the process of shuffling the cards, said, "You can bet up to three dollars before the draw, five dollars after. There's a quarter ante; we don't take more than five percent of any pot as a house cut, and if you're on the button, you have to bet three dollars blind, but is a live blind."

A yellow disk or button was moved around the table, representing the theoretical dealer, since only the house dealer dealt the cards; whoever was to the left of the button was the first to bet and had to bet $3 in the blind. Thereafter, when the bettting came back to him, he could raise. That was what a live blind meant.

Only the house dealer handled the cards. He shuffled them, cut them himself, and then began dealing, starting with the player to the left of the button.

There was a $20 buy-in, which meant that I had to have at least $20 on the table before I could play the game. I cashed in $100 so as to have some money in front of me; the game was table stakes, and you couldn't dip into your pocket during the betting. I got $1 and $5 casino checks and a bunch of quarters for my antes.

I threw in a quarter, and the game was on. The first hand I was dealt was kings up, an absolute bust in lowball. I threw them away and looked over my fellow players.

Three of them wore cowboy hats, three others were older men who seemed to know each other, calling each other by their first names, and the other player was a young man in his early twenties, looking a little out of his element, wearing a torn plaid shirt and nervously rearranging his quarters, clinking them loudly.

On the first deal three players stayed in for the draw, one drew two cards, one drew one card, and the man who had bet blind drew three cards.

I was amazed that any player except the blind bettor would draw more than one card. You just couldn't do that in lowball and survive.

On the next deal I was again dealt a bust. I watched the game, trying to separate the weak players from the strong. Now there were five players in before the draw, and there had been one raise during the first round of betting, yet two of the players were drawing two cards again. I just couldn't believe my eyes. Was this

84

really five-card draw, lowball? It sure was.

I became really interested in this game. I was playing with a bunch of terrible players. One fellow with a cowboy hat had twice drawn one card, yet he had raised before the draw on the last hand. This game seemed incredible.

I had studied poker and made a good living from it in the East, and while I had hardly any opportunity to play five-card draw, lowball, I knew the principles clearly. You couldn't draw to more than one card, and if you did, you needed a 7-high hand or lower. But these players were drawing to 10-high hands, were drawing two cards, and were raising on nothing. It was truly incredible.

After five deals I was to the left of the button. I bet $3 in the blind and looked at my cards. I held 7 5 3 2 A. A pat hand. When three players called, I raised on my turn, and they all called my raise.

Two drew two cards, and the third player drew one card. I stood pat. It was my bet. I bet $5, and the one who drew a single card called. The others folded, as I guessed they would. What could you buy with a two-card draw in lowball except heartaches? I showed my 7 5 high, and the player conceded, but he threw his cards face up on the table, muttering to a fellow crony that he couldn't win with anything tonight. He held a 9 8 high hand. Another sucker.

The game droned on. I played according to my principles, staying in with only pat hands or one-card draws to 7-high hands. Liquor was continually being served at the table, and some of the players were really getting drunk and looser in their play.

I had more coffee. Two of the players, both heavy losers, were getting downright nasty, accusing friends of playing too tightly, of never taking chances. I half expected them to turn on me, but I was a stranger in the game, and they left me alone.

I continued to win my share of the pots. No matter how tightly I played, I had my group in with me both before and after the draw. I beat out one cowboy who went in after the draw with deuces against my pat hand. It was like taking candy from babies.

A few players finally quit the game, but others moved into their seats. A man in his forties sat down, but he was as poor as the player he replaced. A red-bearded man also sat down, and he played a good game. By four in the morning only two of the original group were left, two drunken cowboys. Of the other players my only competition was the man with the red beard, who played a good, tight game.

I was now ahead almost $200. For about two hours after reaching this plateau, I just couldn't get good cards, and my winnings dwindled slightly. The red-bearded player had a good run and was piling up the chips in front of him.

At this point I was so tired that I decided to leave the game, but I wanted to stay for one more round of play since I was about to be the first player to bet, the one under the gun, and it seemed penny ante to leave before I bet blind. I was fingering about $150 in winnings at this time.

When I was under the gun, I bet $3 in the blind, not even looking at my cards. The cowboy who was drunkest and had taken an awful beating in the game raised me without looking at his cards. Another player called the raise, and then the rebearded player reraised him. I looked at my cards. I held 6 5 3 2 A, wonderful low cards. Only a 6 4 and a wheel could beat me.

I reraised the bearded player, and the cowboy faded out, but the other player called my reraise. The redhead came back with another raise, I reraised, and the other player called. When the rehead wanted to reraise, he was told we had reached our limit of raises, so he called.

I stood pat, the redhead stood pat, and the third player took one card for his draw. I couldn't believe his move, but I was now worried about the redhead's hand.

I was first to bet, so I threw in $5, the redhead raised, and the other player folded. I reraised, and he reraised, and I reexamined my cards.

I'ts possible, I thought, that he has me beat. He could have the 6 4 or the wheel. Anything was possible, but highly improbable.

I reraised, and then the bearded player turned to the dealer.

"How many raises are we allowed?" he asked.

"With two players, it's table stakes. You can bet all you have in front of you if you want."

The redhead looked at me. He had a freckled face, long eyelashes, and a slightly florid complexion, he was in his late twenties or early thirties, wearing a semi-Western sports shirt.

"What do you say?" he asked me.

"About what?"

He counted his chips. "I've got $220 here," he said.

I said nothing.

"You want to call my $220 bet?"

"Maybe," I said.

"Yes or no?"

"Bet it," I said.

He shoved in all his chips. I could feel my heart pound as I watched his hand, steadily moving in the chips. Well, this would take all my money to call; at worst, I'd lose my original $100.

I hesitated for an instant. He stared at me, confident, his eyes bright, his demeanor composed. The bastard might have that wheel, I thought; he's got me screwed. Still, I had a great hand, a hand equivalent to four of a kind in high poker. Now or never.

I counted out my chips and shoved them in, leaving myself with a couple of dollar chips and some quarters.

"What do you have?" he asked.

"I'm calling you."

My adversary put down his hand face up. 6 5 4 2 A.

I put down my cards. 6 5 3 2 A. He stared at me with a shocked expression. Did he think I played like those cowboys?

The whole pile of chips were shoved over to me. It took a while to stack them up and carry them away. There was no point in staying any longer. The redhead, tapped out, got up to leave, heading for the front door while I headed for the cashier's cage.

After I folded away the hundred-dollar bills, I headed out toward my car. It was bright out; the sun was shining with blinding intensity. My car hadn't been disturbed. I drove down to the Strip, stopped off for another breakfast, and bought a paper; later that morning, I took an apartment near the Strip, using my winnings for the deposit and first month's rent.

It was the beginning of a year's stay in Vegas. I went back a few times to that original poker game, but the players had changed. I never had that same good feeling I had had that wild night, when, bleary-eyed, I had taken my measure of the cowboys and the man with the red beard.

Five-Card Stud, Lowball

This game is played the same way as high five-card stud, with two major exceptions. First, flushes and straights don't count; second, the lowest hand wins. All the other rules are the same as to dealing and number of rounds played.

Number of Players

Two to ten can play, but the best game is with six to eight players.

Rank of the Cards

See Lowball Poker, Rank of Cards.

Rank of Hands

Again, see Lowball Poker, Rank of Hands. I'm going to show as an illustrative game one that I was involved in as the Fourth Player. The game was a $1-$10 game, not a usual betting game because of the wide swing.

There were eight players in the game, and it was held in a private residence, so there was no house rake or ante. Like most stud-poker games five-card stud, lowball usually doesn't require an ante if there are sufficient players in the game.

In the course of this game I'll show my own hole card, but all other hole cards will be shown by an *.

First Betting Round. Here are the holdings before the first round of betting.

Player	Hand
First:	* 8
Second:	* 6
Third:	* K
Fourth:	A A
Fifth	* Q
Sixth:	* 9
Seventh:	* 5
Dealer:	* 3

88

I was the Fourth Player and had to open with the ace because in this version of stud poker lowest card opens the betting; on the first round of betting, the best card must open the betting.

Since I was already paired, which was bad, I opened with a $1 bet, preparing to fold my cards when I was raised. However, everyone except the Third and Fifth Players saw my bet. Six players remained in the game, and there was $6 in the pot.

Second Betting Round. Here are the holdings:

Player	Hand
First:	* 8 7
Second:	* 6 J
Fourth:	A A 3
Sixth:	* 9 Q
Seventh:	* 5 10
Dealer:	* 3 6

I was still sick of my cards because of that ace pair, and I felt that anyone who could get to the showdown with the unmatched cards was going to beat me easily. I wanted to steal the pot now and bet $5. It wasn't the lowest or the highest bet I could make, and it didn't make much of an impression on the others because only the Second and Sixth Players folded. There was now $26 in the pot.

Third Betting Round. Here are the holdings:

Player	Hand
First:	* 8 7 9
Fourth:	A A 3 5
Seventh:	* 5 10 10
Dealer:	* 3 6 2

These cards were amazing. I was getting better and better cards, and although the Seventh Player's buy destroyed his hand, the other players were getting wonderful cards also. I wouldn't be able to shake them, but I felt a check now would be the worst thing I could do. I decided to try and pull the hand out.

So I slid out $10 and bet it. The Seventh Player folded, which was no surprise, and the Dealer called, as did the First Player, rather reluctantly, I noted. There was now $56 in the pot.

Fourth and Final Betting Round. Here are the holdings:

Player	Hand
First:	* 8 7 9 9
Fourth:	A A 3 5 8
Dealer:	* 3 6 2 K

My cards were getting better and better! The First Player was already folding his cards when I bet $10 quickly. I had bet with impunity, but I was beaten if the Dealer called my hand.

But how could he call? He couldn't beat my cards on board, and his king buy had weakened his hand considerably. If I held any unmatched card lower than the king as my hole card, he was done for.

He thought for a while, looking at my face, then at my cards; then he folded his cards, and I took the pot. I turned over my ace for the table's benefit to show that I was capable of bluffing and didn't always play that tight a hand.

As I gathered in the cash, I knew that the Dealer was cursing himself for not staying in and calling with five matched cards.

Strategy in Five-card Stud, Lowball

The most important thing to consider is that in this five-card game there is little margin for error. You only get five cards, and any one of them can destroy your hand. You can buy a pair or a face card, and there's nothing you can do to prevent or conceal it unless you pair a low card in your hand with the hole card.

When playing this game, you have to sweat out each buy. For this reason, it's a game that should be played for high stakes or for stakes with a wide swing between low and high bets. If you're unable to drive out the other players with big bets and raises, there's nothing you can do but stay in round after round and pray for good luck.

The more rounds you stay in, the more chances you have of disaster striking your hand. You can show a 4 3 A in your board cards and then get another 4, and suddenly your hand is kaput.

Therefore, two strategies have to be followed. You have to go in with low cards, no higher than 7, at the outset and bet the limit to try and drive everyone else out. Or force them to go along with your big bets so long as you are top man.

Generally speaking, if you can last to the end with an un-matched hand, you've a chance of winning, and even a hand headed by a middling card such as 8, 9 or 10 will win for you. But don't go in with these cards at the outset. Limit your involvement on the first two cards to hand containing no card above a 7.

Since the brutal fact of this game is that one card can wreck any hand, there's an extra element of luck involved in this game that's not involved in other forms of lowball poker. Many gamblers prefer to play razz, the seven-card lowball stud game, or draw power, lowball, where they won't be on the edge of their seats with every buy, praying that their hand doesn't get bombed out with one bad card.

Seven-Card Stud, Lowball

This is a much better game than the five-card version of stud lowball because each player is dealt seven cards and uses the five best to form his hand, so one bad buy won't ruin his holding.

The game is called razz when played in the Nevada casinos.

In seven-card stud, lowball the same rules that prevail in regular high seven-card stud apply, with two basic exceptions. First, flushes and straights don't count; second, the lowest hand is the best hand.

For ranking of cards and hands, see *Lowball Poker*.

Number of Players

Two to nine can play, but the best game is with six to eight players.

Let's follow a typical game of seven-card stud, lowball. There are 7 players in the game, and the game is a $5-$10 one.

There is no ante; on the opening round the player with the lowest-ranking card must open the betting. For betting and playing purposes in lowball poker the ace is always the lowest card, having a ranking equivalent to a 1.

All hole cards are represented by the symbol *.

First Round of Betting. Here are the holdings before the first round of betting:

Player	Hand
First:	* * 9
Second:	* * J
Third:	* * Q
Fourth:	* * 2
Fifth:	* * 2
Sixth:	* * 6
Dealer:	* * 7

The Fourth Player is low, having bought the first deuce. He bets $5, since he must open. The Fifth and Sixth Players call, as does the Dealer. The First, Second, and Third Players fold. There is $20 in the pot.

Second Round of Betting. Here are the holdings:

Player	Hand
Fourth:	* * 2 10
Fifth:	* * 2 3
Sixth:	* * 6 A
Dealer:	* * 7 K

The Fifth Player, with his nice 3 2 holding, is low. He bets $5. The Sixth Player raises to $10. The Dealer folds, but the Fourth Player calls the $10 bet, and the Fifth Player calls the raise. There is now $50 in the pot.

Third Round of Betting. Here are the holdings:

Player	Hand
Fourth:	* * 2 10 7
Fifth:	* * 2 3 2
Sixth:	* * 6 A J

Only the Fourth Player improved his hand on this round, and he finds himself low man. He bets $10. The Fifth and Sixth Players, whose buys hurt them, call the bet. There is $80 in the pot.

Fourth Round of Betting. Here are the holdings:

Player	Hand
Fourth:	* * 2 10 7 8
Fifth:	* * 2 3 2 Q
Sixth:	* * 6 A J 4

The Fourth Player is still low and bets $10. The Fifth Player, who has now absorbed two bad buys, find that his hand is valueless and folds. The Sixth Player raises to $20.

The Fourth Player looks over the raiser's hand and finds that he must respect that 6 A and 4 showing. He calls the bet and hopes for the best: $120 is in the pot.

Fifth and Last Round of Betting. Here are the holdings:

Player	Hand
Fourth:	3 6 2 10 7 8 J
Sixth:	4 2 6 A J 4 K

The Fourth Player holds an 8 7 high hand, but he still must respect the board cards of the Sixth Player and doesn't know that the hole cards of the opponent have destroyed his hand.

Since the Fourth Player can't see through closed cards, he checks. The game is a limit game, with only a $10 maximum bet; the Sixth Player knows that if he bets $10, he's going to be called and will lose the pot and the extra $10, so he checks also. Both players turn over their cards and the Fourth Player wins the pot.

If this had been a higher-limit game or a pot-limit game, after the Fourth Player's check, the Sixth Player, because of his good three-card board holding, might have attempted to steal the pot with a bluff, but he had no chance here.

Strategy in Seven-Card Stud, Lowball

Again, the best strategy is to go in with good cards and only good cards before the first betting round. It's best to stay in with three odd cards, the highest being a 7. This is the recommendation of a former world champion, Johnny Moss, and I wholeheartedly agree with his philosophy.

If you stay in with only a 7-high card (or lower), you'll have fighting cards to the end, with a good chance of winning the pot.

Even though your hand can be easily ruined by bad buys, you want to stay in with the very best cards possible to absorb one bad buy in the hope of getting a better hand. If you stay in, however, with mediocre cards, and one bad buy will end your chances of winning, you're playing bad poker.

When you play this tightly, you won't be in on many hands, but those you'll be playing will pay off for you because you'll be the favorite to win at the showdown.

If you don't want to get a reputation as a very, very tight player, go in with an 8-high holding occasionally, but that's it.

Don't start with higher cards, or they'll cost you money.

When you have the best hand, you must make the others pay heavily to stay in with you. You must start raising from the outset and punish the opponents.

Seven-card stud, lowball is not a game to play possum in because of the uncertainty in buying good cards. A strong hand can fade quickly by the end with a couple of bad cards, and so you must try to get the other players out or to call your big bets with inferior cards. In the long run this strategy will work well because while you may get a bad buy, so may they, and your cards are lower than theirs, and you'll still have the advantage.

It's a simpler game than seven-card stud, high because here we're just concerned with low hands, and that's all, whereas in seven-card stud those hole cards can hide all kinds of big powerful hands.

So to sum up: Stay in with three odd cards, with the highest no larger than a 7, bet big when you have the goods, and you'll do all right.

Razz, The Casino Game

Once a very popular game in the Nevada casinos, it is rarely played these days. The games I've seen in the casino poker rooms have generally been played for medium to high stakes.

The main difference between the private and casino game is that in the casino game high card is forced to open the betting, not low card. This is done to keep more players in and enhance the pots.

If you play in the casino game, play the same tight game you'd play in a private game. If you are forced to open because you're high man, get right out the next round, and don't chase that opening bet.

7. HIGH-LOW POKER

Introduction

High-low has become a very popular game because of the big pots generated and the chance to share part of the pot, holding either a high or low hand.

High-low means just what it says: In this form of poker both the high and low hands have equal value, and players may go for either the highest or the lowest hand or for both high and low at the same time. All the high-low games discussed in this book will be games where the players declare or call their hands, rather than games in which the cards "speak for themselves."

High-low can be played as draw or stud poker in many variations, but the best game is seven-card stud, in which there is more of a chance to make both high and low hands at the same time.

In the five-card games such as draw or five-card stud usually each player can only make a high or low hand, but in seven-card stud, in which there are seven cards to choose from to form two best hands, a player may have both the high and low hand at the same time.

At the showdown a player may call or declare high or low or high-low. If he calls high and has the highest-ranking hand, he wins half the pot. If he calls low and has the lowest-ranking hand, he wins half the pot. He calls high-low and has both the highest and lowest-ranking hands, he wins the whole pot.

Should all the participants at the showdown declare low, the lowest-ranking hand wins the whole pot, and the same principle holds true if all the players declare high.

If a player calls high-low, he must have both high hand and low hand; otherwise, the cards he holds are worthless. Should there be players calling both high and low, and one player calls high-low and has the highest-ranking hand but not the lowest-ranking hand, he forfeits his chance to win a portion of the pot, and his hand is dead. Now the highest-ranking hand of those calling high take one-half the pot, along with the lowest-ranking hand of those calling low.

To repeat, in order to win if you call high-low, you must have both the highest-and lowest-ranking hands. If you have one without the other, you forfeit the pot and are out of contention.

To illustrate, let's follow the call at the showdown of five players in seven-card stud, high-low.

Player	Hand	Call
First:	K K 9 9 2 3 10	High
Second:	4 4 4 J 8 5 2	High
Third:	8 6 5 4 2 K Q	Low
Fourth:	7 6 5 2 A Q 9	Low
Fifth:	A A 6 6 7 4 3	High-Low

The highest hand on board belongs to the Second Player, who holds three 4s. The lowest hand belongs to the Fifth Player, who holds a 7 6 4 high hand.

However, since the Fifth Player called high-low, he needs both the highest hand and the lowest hand to win. He has only the lowest hand, and so he loses both and is out of contention. The Second Player collects his half of the pot for the high hand, and the Fourth Player collects his half of the pot for low hand with his 7 6 5 2 A holding.

Draw Poker, High-Low
Number of Players
Two to eight, with six to eight the best game.

In many high-low games there will be more players staying in to the end since either a low hand or a high hand can win half the pot.

The standard deck of 52 cards is used, and the game is played exactly as high or low draw poker. If a player goes for a high hand, straights and flushes count. If he goes for a low hand, straights and flushes don't count, the ace is considered the lowest-ranking card, and a wheel (5 4 3 2 A) is the best low hand.

A big difference between draw poker, high-low and other forms of draw poker is the showdown. All the players, after the final betting is over, declare whether or not they are going for high or low or both high-low before they show their cards.

If the game is played with different-colored chips, then the best way to declare is to hold a chip in your hand, white for low, blue for high, and red for high-low. Coins can also be used. A penny signifies a low call, a dime a high call, and a nickel, high-low. These are just suggestions, but any manner in which everyone calls at the same time is correct. At one time all players open their hands to show their call.

By the statement "opening their hands" I am referring to the anatomical hand, not the card hand. If players don't call at one time but in succession, there will be an inequitable advantage to the last callers since they can take advantage of previous calls. For example, if there are four players left at the showdown, and the first three have called low, the fourth player can simply call high, no matter what his hand, and win half the pot.

A player in high-low is bound by his call. If he calls low but has the high hand, he cannot win the high half of the pot. If he calls either high or low and has won both high and low, he can only claim the part of the pot he called, not the whole pot.

In draw poker, high-low the game is anything opens, not jacks or better.

All draw-poker games should be played with an ante to keep the players in and to sweeten the pot. There usually is more betting and raising in high-low since a player with a winning hand at either high or low wants his share of the pot to be rather rich, and he will raise with impunity.

For example, there are five players in the game after the draw. Player A holds 6 4 3 2 A, a sure winner at low. He has stood with a pat hand. The other three players have drawn two and three cards, obviously going for high hands. Another player bets. Player A now raises the limit, and since he is figured for a low hand (rarely are there pat hands in high draw poker), the other players, who must go for their high calls and half of the pot, have no other recourse but to see the raise if they feel they have a chance to win the high share of the pot.

On the other hand, if you've drawn two cards to triplets and gotten a full house, you again raise the limit, knowing your half of the pot is secure because of your powerful hand. You do this even if one player has stood pat and the other two are drawing one card apiece. Whether they're going for high or low, you should still win half the pot.

A good variation in betting, which increases the tension and the pot markedly, is to have one final betting round after the call.

For example, let's say four players are in on the showdown. All the betting rounds have been completed, and the players now call. Two call high, and two call low. With this variation, another betting round follows.

If one player feels he has a lock on either the high or low hand, he'll bet or raise the limit, forcing the other two players going for the opposite half of the pot to go along with his bet or raise.

If only three players are left at the showdown, and one calls high and two call low, then the high hand takes out his half of the pot, and the other two have another betting round, fighting for the pot that remains. This is done to prevent the sole hand calling high to force the others to increase his share of the pot when, in reality, he has no competition for that share.

Should four players remain at the showdown, and two call high, one low and one-high-low, the low hand cannot claim half the pot since he is challenged by the high-low caller. After another round of betting, in which all participate, the cards are shown and the winners determined.

In draw poker, high-low it is rare for a player to win both the high and low hands, but it is possible. A player may have a low straight, such as 6 5 4 3 2, which will win the high bet, and since straights don't count in determining the low-hand winner, he calls a 6 5 hand to take the other half of the pot as well.

A low flush can also with both ways, with a hand such as ♦7 ♦5 ♦4 ♦2 ♦A. It is considered an ace-high flush for high, and since flushes don't count in low poker, it is simply a 7 5 hand, which would have an excellent chance of winning at draw poker, lowball.

Of course, in both instances, the player would have to call high-low.

Strategy in Draw Poker, High-Low

The best strategy I can recommend is to stay in only with cards that can win, whether you are going for the high or low hand. Examine the staying-in strategy for both high and low draw poker in their respective sections before you play this game.

For example, in the high variation you'd want at least kings or aces as a minimum hand before the draw; in the low variation you wouldn't want to draw more than one card to a 7-high hand.

The other basic strategy in high-low is to determine just what kinds of hands the other players are playing for, whether they are going for high or low hands. High-low hands occur so rarely that they shouldn't be a pertinent consideration.

When a player draws two or three cards, you can be sure he's going for a high hand unless he's an utter fool. The difficulty comes on the one-card draws. A one-card draw can mean two pairs or a four flush or straight in high poker, or it can mean, just as easily, a player going for a low hand, holding four odd cards.

One must therefore be very alert in this game. There will be many times when you can correctly gauge other players' hands, but there will be times when they will remain a mystery.

For example, a player may draw one card and then raise a player who's drawn two cards. The player drawing two cards may have gone in with three of a kind as a high hand. The player drawing one card might have drawn a flush or a straight and now holds the upper hand in high poker. Or he may have drawn to a low hand and bought a low odd card with a good chance at low poker.

That is why it is so important to begin with good cards for your respective hand, whether it be high or low. Otherwise, you may be wiped out by a series of raises between two players ready to call one way, while you, with mediocre cards, have to call the same way. Or both players may have a lock on each side, one high and one low, and you don't stand a chance either way. It's a dangerous and exciting game, and the best strategy is staying in only with top cards.

Five-Card Stud, High-Low

In five-card stud, high-low the hands players are going for, either high or low, can be pretty obvious.

Five-card stud is rarely played as a high-low game anymore, but if you are involved in five-card stud, high-low, the best rule to follow is to play tight, very tight. Then play for either a high or low hand, not for both because both hardly ever develop in such a limited game.

If you play high, follow the strategy outlined in five-card stud, high, and if you go for the low hand, follow the strategy in five-card stud, lowball.

In that way you'll make the most of the hands you have, and though most of the time you'll only collect half the pot, with good cards and proper raises you can make that pot worthwhile.

If you and your friends want a good stud game of high-low, I'd recommend passing up five-card stud and sticking to the seven-card stud game.

Seven-Card Stud, High-Low

This is one of the best poker gambling games, and it's a game where a smart and skillful player can make a lot of money. Because of the three hidden cards the game is very exciting when played as a high-low game, and there is usually plenty of action, plenty of raises, and plenty of weak players staying in to the showdown.

Weak players love this game, and strong players adore it for different reasons. For the weak player there are all those cards to buy, and if the high hand doesn't develop, maybe a low hand will come out of that mess.

The strong player, on the other hand, plays for either high or low, plays tight, stays in only with good cards, makes the most of his hand, and usually has little difficulty separating the weaker players from their money or chips.

Number of Players

Two to nine, with the game best played with six to eight players.

The same deck and the same rules are used as in seven-card stud, high with two exceptions. First, in judging a low hand, straights and flushes don't count. Second, in the low hands the ace is always the lowest-ranking card.

Let's follow a typical seven-card stud game, high-low. Usually, the high card or the high hand bets first, and on the first betting round the highest-ranked card must open the betting. An ace showing is always the highest-ranking card even if the player is going for a low hand. The ace on board speaks for itself as a high card for betting purposes.

There are eight players in this game, and it is a $1-$2 game.

First Round of Betting. The * stands for the hidden card. Here are the holdings before the first round of betting.

Player	Hand
First:	* * 8
Second:	* * 6
Third:	* * K
Fourth:	* * J
Fifth:	* * 2
Sixth:	* * 3
Seventh:	* * A
Eight:	* * 10

The Seventh Player opens with a $2 bet because the ace is boss in this game and can go either way, high or low, with great effect. The Dealer folds since a middling 10 is poison in high-low, and the Fourth Player also folds with his jack, but all the others stay in and call the bet. There's $12 in the pot.

Second Round of Betting. Here are the holdings:

Player	Hand
First:	* * 8 9
Second:	* * 6 4
Third:	* * K Q
Fifth:	* * 2 10
Sixth:	* * 3 A
Seventh:	* * A Q

The Seventh Player is high with his A Q holding, but these cards are neither here nor there in high-low poker, so he checks. Once he checks, he's still in the game, but he can't raise on this round since this is not a check-and-raise game.

The First Player also checks, the Second Player bets $2, and all the other players stay in on this round. Anything is possible. There is now $24 in the pot.

Third Round of Betting. Here are the holdings:

Player	Hand
First:	* * 8 9 8
Second:	* * 6 4 3
Third:	* * K Q K
Fifth:	* * 2 10 Q
Sixth:	* * 3 A J
Seventh:	* * A Q 9

The Third Player, with kings, is high. he bets $2. The Fifth Player, whose cards have been getting progressively worse, folds. The Sixth Player, whose jack buy didn't help his low hand, calls the bet. The Seventh Player folds, having gone for a low hand and watched his cards turn high and go nowhere.

The First Player, with his pair showing, calls, and the Second Player, who has a nice low hand showing, raises the betting by $2 The Third Player now reraises to $6, the Sixth Player calls by betting $4, the First Player also calls with a $4 bet, the Second Player now reraises by $2, and all the others call this raise. There is now $56 in the pot. A one- and two-dollar game of high-low can really escalate into big pots.

Fourth Round of Betting. Here are the holdings:

Player	Hand
First:	* * 8 9 8 K
Second:	* * 6 4 3 3
Third:	* * K Q K 7
Sixth:	* * 3 A J 7

The kings are still high. The 7 was a meaningless buy for the Third Player, and he also notes a king falling into the First Player's hand. Since the Third Player is a weak and cautious player, he decides to check and see what develops. The Sixth Player checks, and the First Player, heartened by the weak check of the Third Player, opens the betting this round with $2 and is immediately raised by the Second Player.

The Third Player shoves in $4, calling the raise, and the Sixth Player also calls the raise, but now the First Player goes up one more time with a $2 raise, and the other three players call this new raise. The pot now holds $76.

Fifth and Final Round of Betting. Here are the holdings:

Player	Hand
First;	* * 8 9 8 K *
Second:	* * 6 4 3 3 *
Third:	* * K Q K 7 *
Sixth:	* * 3 A J 7 *

The kings are still high, but the Third Player checks. The Sixth Player checks; the First Player goes in with a $2 bet and is raised $2 by the Second Player. The Third Player calls the $4 raise, but the Sixth Player has had enough and folds.

The First Player reraises, and the Second Player, seeing that he now has a clear field as to half the pot because of his low holding, raises again, and this costs the Third Player $4 more.

The First Player reraises again, and so does the Second Player, and now the Third Player is caught in the middle. He's played his hand terribly, and his check in an earlier round gave the First Player all the incentive he needed to raise and reraise. Finally, having taken enough punishment, he folds.

This leaves only the First and Second Players in the game to split the pot. The First Player now calls the raise, and calls high, the Second Player calls low at the same time, and they split the pot, which is a sizable $106.

Here's what the holdings looked like on the last round with al the hole cards exposed.

Player	Hand
First:	8 A 8 9 8 K 2
Second:	7 2 6 4 3 3 9
Third:	4 4 K Q K 7 10
Sixth:	7 5 3 A J 7 K

Strategy in Seven-Card Stud, High-Low

In seven-card stud, high-low a player must go for either a high or low hand at the outset and stay in with cards that are appropriate to that hand. If he plays for a high hand, he should stay in with cards that he would stay in with in seven-card stud, high. If he plays for low, he should stay in with those cards that are recommended in the section on seven-card lowball and no others

Don't play purposely for a high-low hand. At times, a hand might develop into a perfect high-low hand, such as an ace-high flush with no other card above a 7 or a low staight to the 5 or 6, but these hands come without playing for them. They develop because strong players stay in with good cards in the first place.

If you have a hand that can be called both high and low, be sure from the betting and the play that you can win both sides; otherwise, your hand is worth nothing if you lose to either a higher or lower hand.

Play the game not as if it is high-low but as a seven-card high or low stud game. If you have the high hand, play it according to the rules of seven-card stud, high, and if you have a low hand, play it as the low version of seven-card stud.

You can make a lot of money in high-low if you play a smart, tight game. It's an ideal game for the skillful player.

8. OTHER POKER GAMES

Games
Iron Cross

In Iron Cross, after the players receive their closed cards, the open cards are laid out on the board to be used as common cards by all the players. The players form their best hands by using a combination of these open cards and their closed cards. All the open cards belong to all the players, and any player may make use of them.

Each player is dealt five cards face down as in draw poker, but there is no draw. Instead, a card is placed face up on each betting round till five cards are laid out in this kind of pattern.

$$X$$
$$X\ X\ X$$
$$X$$

All the participants use these cards in conjunction with their own to form the best possible hand, but they're limited to using three cards either horizontal or vertical.

For example, you hold A K K 3 2, and the board shows:

$$8$$
$$6\ K\ 2$$
$$Q$$

You can either use the 8 K Q, or the 6 K 2.

By making use of the king and deuce on board, you hold a full house. Other players are also utilizing these same board cards to form their hands as well, but your hand is very strong here.

These games lead to wild betting and big play because many players have superstrong hands. Therefore, you must play an extremely tight game and realize that flushes and straights are not that good and will fall to full house or better many times.

This game is also known as Cincinnatti or Crisscross, depending on the region this game is played in.

Six-Card Stud

Six-card stud is a cross between five-card and seven-card stud.

Two cards are dealt closed at the outset with one open; then the first round of betting begins. Altogether there are four rounds of betting, as in five-card stud, but that extra hole card makes a world of difference, making six-card stud a highly exciting game.

To play it well, study the strategies of five-card and seven-card stud. It's in between; play a little looser than five card and a little tighter than seven card and you won't go wrong.

A variation of six-card stud that's popular in the big-money private games is called "guts" and "big sweet", among other names.

The first card is dealt face down, the next four face up, and the final card is face down again. This allows one more betting round since only two cards, instead of three are dealt at the outset.

When played as either a low game, a high game, or a high-low game, one or two extra rounds of betting are allowed. After the final bet is made, any player may replace any card in his hand and receive another card from the stock. If he replaces an open card, he gets an open card. If he replaces a closed card, he gets another closed card.

Then another betting round ensues. In high-low, after this betting round, there is the call, then still another round of betting.

This game can run into astronomical stakes even with a small limit, so I suggest that before you every play it, you know your poker cold. It is one of the most exciting big-pot games around.

Special Features and Plays
Wild Cards

A common feature of many games is the introduction of a wild card, which can be made by the holder of that card into any card he desires. For example, if a joker is wild, and you hold three aces, you can make that joker into a fourth ace. If you have a four flush, the joker becomes that suit, and you have a flush. If you have an open-ended straight, the joker becomes the high card of that straight.

In the California poker clubs the draw poker games have a joker or bug added to the deck, but it has limited value in the high draw games since it can only be used as an ace or to fill in a flush or straight. In this case the joker is a limited wild card.

In private games, usually the joker or any deuce is a wild card when that's a feature of the game. A player can use the wild card as any card or suit. If he holds the deuce of diamonds, and deuces are wild, he can turn that card into the ace of spades if he so wishes.

When playing in games in which deuces are wild, you must remember that there are four wild cards in the game; therefore, hands that would ordinarily win pots will become losers when confronted with a hand containing a wild deuce.

To overcome this, downgrade your hands by one level. If you're playing draw poker, your kings might not be worth a raise on the opening round. There will be many three-of-a-kind hands because of the deuces, and you should count on this kind of hand to win rather than two pair or simply a high pair, such as kings or aces.

To win, you have to re-evaluate your hands and play a tighter game than usual. When you do this, you'll come out all right. Wild cards shouldn't deter the tight, strong player because the game gets looser, with bigger pots and more players staying in to the showdown.

Roll Your Own

This feature is applied to stud-poker games. Instead of one card dealt face up with the closed card or cards, with "roll your own", all cards at the outset are dealt face down, and the player selects which card he chooses to show as a face-up card.

For example, in seven-card stud, high you're dealt ace, ace, 6 face down. You put up the 6 as your face-up card.

This feature makes for bigger pots and more action. In high-low games it can be used to mislead the other players in order to get an edge in the betting and the final call. Suppose a player is dealt 6 5 2 and puts out the 2. His opponents may feel that he's going for a high hand, not a low one, and is concealing two big cards underneath.

Or a player might be dealt K K 5 and put out the king as though he had small cards underneath. This reverse psychology often works. In roll your own, an extra measure of psychological insight helps quite a bit because this variation makes stud poker even more of a thinking man's game than it already is.

Bonuses and Royalties

In some poker games players are rewarded for holding certain top hands by being given a bonus or royalty. Usually the bonus amounts to either the lower or higher limit of the betting range of the particular game. In a $5-$10 game the royalty can be either $5 or $10, as the players agree.

Royalties are usually paid out in high stud games for holdings of a royal flush, straight flush, or four of a kind. These payments have nothing to do with skill but reward the lucky buyer of top cards.

Other Variations and Features

Poker is a dynamic game, and new variations of the basic games are continually being used, as well as new features to make the game even more exciting and worthwhile. It would be impossible to list all the variations because many are local and regional.

What I have attempted to do in this book is present the correct strategies for the basic play of poker so that when you do encounter any feature or variation that is new, your sound background will allow you to handle it easily.

Don't be afraid of these features and variations when they occur. Take advantage of them because they generally mean looser play and bigger pots, and that's the name of the game, isn't it?

9. HOLD 'EM POKER

Introduction

This game, also known as Texas hold'em, has become one of the most popular poker games, and with good reason.

It is a great spectator game, a great action game, a great betting game, and it attracts a lot of players. What more could anyone ask of a poker game? In fact, it has become the most popular of all poker games played in both the California clubs and casinos around the country, pushing aside seven card stud as the number one game.

The game was popularized by Texans, such as the great Doyle "Texas Dolly" Brunson, and certainly by the Horseshoe Club in Downtown Las Vegas, which inaugurated a World Series of Poker some years back, featuring Texas hold'em. As a wide group of poker players saw the potential action in this game, its popularity took off.

Although the game can be played at home, it is primarily a casino or club game, for the average table holds nine or ten players plus a dealer. Playing with less than nine players makes it a short-handed game, and the average home game usually has about five to eight players.

Basics of the Game
Cards

The standard 52-card deck is used, without the jokers.

Object of the Game

To win the pot. This can be done by having the best hand at the showdown or forcing all the other players out of the game so that only one hand remains and takes the pot.

Rank of the Cards

Hold'em is a stud game, and the ace has the highest rank, followed by the king, queen, jack and then the nonface cards in rank from the 10 down to the 2, which has the lowest rank. The suits themselves have no particular rank and are equal.

Rank of the Hands

The same as in high stud poker. See *Fundamental Rules of Poker, Rank of the Hands.*

Number of Players

Two to twenty. The best game is played with either nine or ten players.

Blinds

It is pretty standard today to have two blinds in a hold'em game. A blind is a mandatory bet made by a player prior to receiving cards. Since position is of utmost importance in hold'em, a button moves around the table in a clockwise fashion, signifying the theoretical dealer. It is theoretical, because there is an actual dealer dealing the cards out in the game.

The first player to receive a card, and the first to bet in any round is the player to the left of the button. He becomes the "small blind". The player to his immediate left is the "big blind". Usually, the small blind must bet half the amount of the big blind. For example, in a $10-$20 game, the small blind will bet $5 and the big blind $10. These are mandatory bets.

These are known as "live blinds". In other words, after each other player has bet or folded in turn, either of these blinds can now raise the pot when it is their turn to bet again on the first round.

House Rake

This depends on the particular casino or club and the size of the game. In the California clubs, as a general rule, the rake is taken before the cards are dealt in the smaller games. For example, in a $6-$12 game, with a full table of nine players, with two blinds, one of $2 and one of $6, plus a 50 cent ante, there is

$12.50 on the table. But before the cards are dealt, only $7.50 remains on the table.

In the Nevada and other casinos, there would be no ante in that game, and the blinds would be $3 and $6, with nothing taken off the table till the game was over. Then, a maximum of $2.50 would be removed.

Of course, one of the reasons for the larger rake in the California clubs, in the smaller games, is the "bad beat" jackpot. A jackpot is set up for certain losing hands, such as aces full losing to higher hands. This runs into the thousands of dollars. We'll explain this later.

In the bigger games, there is usually an hourly fee charged to players. It is slightly more in the California clubs than in the Nevada casinos. When there is an hourly fee, there is usually no additional ante required of the players.

The Play of the Game
The Deal

A house employee is the dealer at all times, and he or she shuffles the cards, cuts them and deals without any player touching them. Since position is so important in hold 'em, a button goes around the table, signifying the theoretical dealer. The first player to receive a card is the player to the button's immediate left, the small blind, then the player to his left, the big blind, then everyone else receives a card in order. Each player will hold two cards prior to the first betting round. These are known as "pocket cards".

The first player to act upon his or her hand is the player to the left of the big blind. Let's assume that it's a $10-$20 game, with two blinds out at $5 and $10. The first player to act must either match the $10 blind, raise, or fold. He or she cannot check the hand. Each player has this option in turn, till the betting gets back to the small blind. His blind is live, so he can raise if he wants to, as can the big blind.

To make it perfectly clear, suppose we designate the player to the left of the big blind as player 1. He folds, as does player 2, 3, 4 and 5. But player 6 bets $10, player 7 calls the $10, the small blind folds, but the big blind makes it $20. Now player 6 must call the raise or reraise to stay in action, as must player 7. The big blind is still live and can put in a reraise if raised.

Generally, in the California clubs, only three raises are allowed unless only two players are left in the game. In the Nevada and other casinos, either three or four raises are allowed. The reason for the limitation of raises is to prevent collusion among two players squeezing a third player by unending raises. When only two players are left, there can no longer be collusion, and therefore, the raises are unlimited.

In the course of play, each player will have two cards of his own. He may use both or one of them to make the best possible hand, along with the five cards that will constitute the "board". Or he may use the board itself, without relying on any of his own cards. Thus a player has enormous leeway in forming the best possible hand. As an example, let's suppose that he held Ace 9. The final board showed 7 8 Ace 10 Jack, of various suits. By using the 9 from his hand he has a jack-high straight. That would be his best possible hand.

Eventually, as we will see, there will be three distinct rounds in which cards are dealt to form the board. Each of these rounds will cause a round of betting, so that there will be four rounds of betting altogether. The first round, as we have seen, occurs after each player is dealt two cards.

After the initial round of betting is completed, the dealer "burns" one card by dropping it face down in front of him and then turns over three cards at once. This is known as the "flop".

After the flop is shown, a betting round ensues. Since hold'em games are structured in two tiers, one double the other, such as $1-$2, $3-$6, $5-$10, etc. the betting continues in the lower mode. Thus, in our $10-$20 game, the betting is still at a $10 level on the flop. In our game, the big blind bets first, followed by Player 6 and Player 7. The position never changes during a game of hold 'em.

When the flop is shown and on all subsequent rounds of betting, a player may check if no betting has occurred before he checks. Only before the flop must a player bet or fold.

After this round of betting is over, and assuming two or more players are still in the game, a fourth card is dealt by the dealer after burning a card. This is known as "Fourth Street" or the "turn". Another betting round ensues, and then if at least two players are still in the game, a final card is dealt to the board. This is "Fifth Street" or the "river". At this point, the board is complete, and the board belongs to all the players, since they are community cards. This is a unique aspect of hold'em and determines most of the strategical principles of the game.

Now there is another bet, and then a showdown. The player called shows his hand, and the other players may show or concede. If they show their cards, the best hand wins the pot.

Suppose the final board looked like this:

$$\diamond K \quad \spadesuit 8 \quad \diamond 4 \quad \heartsuit 6 \quad \diamond 7$$

The big blind, who was called, puts down an Ace and 10 of diamonds, giving him an ace-high flush. The other two players concede and throw away their cards.

Unlike other poker games, in hold'em, any player may ask to see the losing hands before they are "mucked", or discarded. This is done rarely, but it is done. The reason for this is simple: in hold'em, you never see the opponents' cards unless he reveals them at the showdown. Thus, with this rule, players get an idea of how a player operates; whether he is wild or conservative, whether he is a bluffer or a tight player.

As mentioned before, position is very important. This is doubly so because the position always remains constant. If you are last to bet on the first round, before the flop, you will always be last to bet in any subsequent round. Conversely, if you are first to bet, you cannot change your position during the remaining rounds of betting.

Since you don't see other players' cards, often you'll judge their strength by the board and by the way they bet. In some cases, position alone can win no matter what cards you hold. For example, suppose the flop came up:

$$\spadesuit 9 \quad \spadesuit 3 \quad \spadesuit 7$$

You are last to bet on the flop. There are three other players in against you, including the big blind. You had raised prior to the flop, and been called by the others. Now they all check to you, and you bet. They may all fold and give you the pot. They're all worried about a spade flush, or perhaps that you hold a pair of aces, one of them being a spade.

If you were in early position when you raised, and bet at the flop, and then someone raised behind you, you're in a difficult position now. This player may have made his flush already, and if you hold two red kings, you're a huge underdog.

Before going on to strategy, let's review the betting procedures in hold'em. After each player receives two cards, his pocket cards, there is a betting round, commencing with the player to the left of the big blind, who must match that bet or raise. Both blinds are live and can raise or reraise when it is their turn to bet.

After the flop is shown, the betting is in sequence, with the small blind, if he remains in the game, first to act. On this round the betting is still at the lower of the two levels, and a player may check when it is his turn to bet, as long as no one bet before him on this round.

On the turn, the betting shifts to the higher level. Thus in a $5-$10 game, it would now be $10 and increments of $10 for raises. On the river, there is another betting round again at the higher level, and then a showdown if more than one player remains in the game. The player called shows his cards first, and the other players may show their cards or concede the hand. If any player so requests, the losing player must show his cards to the table.

A player may use both his or her cards to form the best hand, or may use one card. Or, in some cases, a player may simply use the board, which is the best possible hand. For example, suppose a player holds the Queen and Jack of spades. There is only one spade on board, the eight, and the other cards can't form a flush. The board is as follows:

$$\clubsuit Q \quad \blacklozenge J \quad \heartsuit 10 \quad \clubsuit 9 \quad \spadesuit 8$$

The player's best hand is the board, showing a queen-high straight. But he may still lose to a player holding a king, who would have a king-high straight. The "nuts", or absolute best hand would be an ace-high straight, if any player held both an ace and king.

The Nuts

In hold'em, unlike other poker games, a player can get the nuts, the absolute best hand. For example, if no pairs are on the board, and there are four hearts, such as king 8 6 2 and you hold the Ace of hearts, you have the nut flush. If there are no pairs, and no possibility of a flush (no more than two of any suit showing) and the board shows queen jack 10 and you hold the ace and king, you have the nut straight.

The reason for this prevalence of absolutely best hands is the fact that the cards in hold 'em are community cards, belonging to all the players, who use them to form their best hands.

Check and Raise

In all casino and club games, check and raise is permitted. What this means is that a player can check his hand and then later raise. For example, suppose that on the river, the first player to bet checks, and then another player bets and the next player to act calls. The player that checked originally is permitted to now raise. Or, if there had been a call and raise, he can reraise.

Check and raise is a valuable tool for a good player, if not used too much. Knowing that you may check and then raise puts a little extra fear into other players who may be hesitant to throw in a bet. It is also a valuable tool in the event you want a "free card", that is, a card dealt after a betting round in which there is no bet. This is important when you have a "drawing hand", a hand that needs help to win, such as a four-flush or four-straight. Being an underdog in this situation makes a free card a valuable plus for you.

Strategy

The most important fact to remember in hold'em is that everyone has the same five cards on board to form their own best hands. These five cards are open to all the players, and the same cards you're using to complete your hand are being used by all the other players to complete theirs.

With this in mind, it is of the utmost importance to evaluate your position at the table and to stay in with solid cards before the flop comes up. Since you're only going to be dealt two cards, you'll find long runs of unplayable hands that must be thrown away. Don't worry about getting rid of cards. Be patient. Of all the poker games, the game of hold 'em requires the most patience.

There is a tendency among weak players to play poor to average hands just to see the flop. After all, they see three cards at one time, and those three cards could form any kind of hand. Even if a player went in with a 3 and 2 "offsuit", that is of two different suits, one of the weakest hands you can be dealt, the flop might come up 2 2 2 or 3 3 3 or Ace 4 5. But hoping for these miracle flops is the sure way to lose a lot of money at hold'em. The odds against them are prohibitive, and finally, when you get such a flop such as 2 2 2 or 3 3 3, you might find no one else staying in with such scare cards. Trips on board are indeed scary cards and most players are reluctant to call a bet against them.

Playable Hands

So, our first strategical principle is to determine what cards to play. From any position on the table, the following cards are absolutely the best to hold before the flop and are worth a raise or reraise. They are:

1. Aces
2. Kings
3. Ace and king of the same suit.
4. Ace and king offsuit.

With these cards you are in a position to dominate the game. With aces and kings, even without any more help on board, you may end up a winner. With ace and king of the same suit, you have a flush draw besides the prospect of getting either an ace or king on board. If you do get either card, your "kicker", that is, the other card in your hand not paired will be the best if another player also has the same pair. There is another reason to raise, especially with aces. The more hands remaining to see the board, the weaker are your chances of winning, since the board nearly always presents a prospect of a flush or straight, or someone will get two pair to beat you. This can happen if you allow a big blind to stay in with a 7 3 offsuit when you hold aces and the final board looks like this: 9 7 3 Queen 2.

> 5. Queens
> 6. Jacks

These hands are strong, and worth a raise before the flop but not a reraise. If there is already a raise, a player may have a pair of aces or kings, or ace king, and if the flop comes up: Ace 5 5, for example, your queens or jacks may already be doomed. Your two pair will be weaker than aces over 5s. If both an ace or king come up on the board after an initial raise before the flop, the chances are that you are already badly beaten. The most prevalent card held by any player will be an ace; the next most popular card will be the king.

> 7. A Q, A J, A 10, all suited.
> 8. A Q, A J, A 10, unsuited.

The suited hands give you the possibility of a flush draw, while the unsuited ace holdings give you the chance of an ace on board with a high kicker. In middle or late position these hands are worth a raise before the flop. By middle to late position, I mean being the third player or later to bet after the big blind.

> 9. All pairs from 10s on down to 2s.

Generally, these pairs will not hold up by themselves without help. By help, I mean another card of the same rank to make trips. I would play them against one raise to see the flop, for if you get trips, you will probably win a big hand with the right cards on board. For example, suppose you go in with a pair of 8s, and the flop shows:

♥ J ♣ 8 ♠ A

There had been a raise before the flop but from a late position player. He might just be playing his position, and likely holds an ace with a kicker. If it is a jack, better for you, for you'll get a lot of action. If the final board looks like this:

♥ J ♦ 8 ♠ A ♣ 5 ♠ 2

You pretty much have a winner here with your trips, and you've gotten action from the holder of the ace. If two players hold an ace, even better for you.

With a small pair, tens or lower, if you don't improve on the flop and a queen or higher card shows with active betting, I wouldn't wait around any longer, but would dump the cards.

> ### 10. K Q, K J, K 10, Q J, Q 10, J 10, all suited.

These are strong cards, with possibilities of flushes and straights coming up on board. Their one weakness is the absence of an ace in the hand. Thus a board such as:

♣ 8 ♥ 4 ♦ A ♠ Q ♦ 2

Without a flush draw out there, and you holding king and queen or queen and jack, there is a strong possibility that someone has an ace (about 80%) and your pair of queens are doomed.

Since you aren't holding a pair, you essentially have drawing cards, and if you don't improve either with a high pair or a flush or straight, you'll probably be a loser.

However, if you do get a straight using both hole cards, it will be the nut straight even with a jack 10 holding.

> ### 11. K Q, K J, K 10, Q J, Q 10, J 10, unsuited.

Without the possibility of a flush draw, these hands are basically drawing hands for a straight. But if you get the straight using both hole cards, it will be the nuts.

12. Suited connected cards, 10-9, 9-8, 8-7, 7-6 and 6-5.

These are well hidden cards, which can give you a middling straight, and a flush draw. The flush draw may not be that strong, because at best you might have a 10 high flush, with another player holding superior cards in the same flush. This is particularly true if four of the suit show on board. But without more than one raise before the flop, these cards are playable, and you can win some big hands with them because of their deceptive nature. Most players hold big cards, and no one may put you on a 6-5 if the board shows 3 Ace 4 2 Queen, without a flush draw. You have the nuts here, and might get action from someone holding an ace or a pair of queens, or Ace 5 suited.

13. King x suited. (x = any card)

This hand is playable without a raise, and is better in late position. What you're hoping for is to pair the king and the other card, or to get a flush out of the board. I wouldn't take a raise to play these cards.

14. All other hands.

I would avoid any other hand. It will only get you in trouble. Sometimes a hand such as king-9 or queen-8 unsuited looks good, but the cards are at each end of a straight (king-queen-jack-10-9.) Should you get the perfect board for the straight, you're a loser if someone holds an ace-king.

By being patient and playing only those hands recommended, you're on your way to becoming a strong player at hold'em.

About the big blind. If you're the big blind, and the pot isn't raised, you'll play any two cards you've been dealt. If the pot has been raised, don't "protect your blind" by calling the raise with bad cards. In each subsequent round you'll be the first to act, and with poor cards, all you can do is lose money.

If you're the small blind, or the button, and the pot hasn't been raised, you can stay on weaker cards, such as two to a straight, unsuited. For example, suppose you're on the button, and no one has raised. Only the small or big blind can raise behind you. If you are holding 8-7 unsuited and there are at least four players in against you, you can see the flop with a bet. There is a chance for a straight here. If the flop doesn't help, get out.

All other factors being equal, the later the position, the weaker the cards you can safely play, and the more often you can put in a raise if no one has raised before you. Your position then helps, for in subsequent rounds you act last, and often by just betting, can win the pot.

Other Strategies

It always pays in poker, no matter what the game, to be aggressive. You want to be the player others fear, so that you can control the game. We discussed check raising as a tool. Use this judiciously to keep the other players off-balance. They won't know if you check whether or not you'll come back with a raise.

The one kind of player you don't want to be is one who just calls others bets or raises. This kind of player is known as a "calling station," and is the easiest to beat. If you're in late position, raise with hands you would call with if you think you're the leader at the time. For example, you hold queen-jack and the flop shows:

♣ Q ♦ 10 ♣ 8

Let's assume that the queen and 8 are clubs. If a player puts in a bet, raise. You have flopped the top pair. Probably the other player holds two clubs, or maybe just the ace of clubs and hopes for two perfect cards. By raising him, you're cutting down his "pot odds", by making him put in more money. At this point, with two cards to go, if he's going for the flush, he's approximately a 2.5-1 dog. By making him put in more money, what the pot will pay him will go down proportionately.

Suppose there's $40 in the pot when he bets $10. If you just call with $10, there's now $60 in the pot for his $10 bet. If you raise, there's $80 in the pot for his $20 bet. And your raise may drive out other players, leaving just you and him. If he doesn't get a club on board, he's now almost a 5-1 underdog. If he checks and you bet, and he calls with a $20 bet, you've forced him to wager $40 with a pot that now holds $120. That is what I mean by cutting down the pot odds.

The good rule is this: If you've got top hand and someone is chasing you with a flush or straight draw, keep raising if you can and force him to put in more money. Conversely, if you've got the drawing hand, then you don't want to be raised. You want to get in as cheap as possible.

However, for the sake of getting a free card, let's assume that you have the two clubs, the ace and 9, and the flop showed the ♣ Q ♦ 10 ♣ 8.

If you were in late position, and a player bet into you, by raising here, and just being called, you may get a free card. Suppose the next card is a 9 of diamonds. This gives you a pair, but you believe you're up against queens. However, the other player now is worried that you might have the jack for a straight, so he checks. You check behind him, and now see the river card for nothing. By doing this, you see two free cards, the turn and the river.

By raising on the cheaper street, the flop, you don't have to bet on the expensive streets, the turn and the river. You've saved two bets of $20. If the river shows a club, great. You've won the pot. If the card is a rag, that is, a dead card for you like the 4 of hearts, you lose but it hasn't cost you that much.

In hold'em, most of the action will occur before the flop and on the flop. By then, you should know where you stand. You can't always tell what the other players are holding, so you must study them, and see just how strong or weak they are. The best way to do this is to see what they show on the showdown. If you see a player always staying in with two of a suit, no matter how weak, such as 7-3, you know this is a weak player. If you see a player always stay in with an ace, no matter what the other card, this is also a weak play.

When bluffing, and bluffing is a big part of hold'em, try and bluff the strong players. Weak players will hang in with any possible chance of improving. Strong players, especially if you hold superior position on them, will respect your bet or raise.

So, when you have what you consider the best hand, make the

others pay to see you. Make all the drawing hands pay. Don't give anyone a free card. When you are drawing to a hand, try and get in as cheaply as possible. And vary your play from time to time.

For example, you might put in an early raise with a jack-ten suited, just so the other players can't read you that easily. Sometimes it can work to devastating effect. Suppose you're pictured as a strong player who raises early on good cards. The others will assume when you put in an early raise that you're probably holding at least ace-jack suited, or a pair of aces, kings or queens, and possibly jacks. The flop comes up as follows:

$$\diamondsuit \ 8 \quad \spadesuit \ 10 \quad \heartsuit \ Q$$

You bet, representing that you have a bigger pair than is showing on board, or at least an ace-king. Let's say you get two callers. The next card is a 10. Now you've made a "set", or trip 10s. You bet, and are raised. Someone else probably has a queen with another card, perhaps queen-ace or queen-king or maybe queen-8 and figures that he has the lead. You can reraise here, figuring your trips are tops. If you're reraised, now you have to worry about a straight, and you should just call. But you have to think of this - why would a player stay in with jack-9 against your early raise? The more logical hand is king-queen or ace-queen. In that actual hand, which I played, the river card was a deuce of clubs and on the showdown, I won with the trip 10s against the queens and 8s. The other player had started with queen-8 suited, to me, not a playable hand after an early raise.

Hold'em is an action game, because of all the possible hands that can be made from the board. There's always a flush or straight lurking, because even a queen-6 can lead to a straight, if you fill in the rest of the cards on the board. Play strong and aggressively when you've got the cards, and hold'em should reward you very well.

Above all, be patient. Wait for the cards we recommend you start with before the flop. If you don't get them, keep folding. Sooner or later you'll get the hand you want. But don't play trash or rags. Stick with the playable hands.

10. CALIFORNIA CLUB POKER

Introduction

California has a long history of card clubs. At one time the only games permitted were draw poker and its variations, such as high and low draw. Those games were played without a house dealer, with players dealing the cards themselves. There were intricate rules for these games, and the hapless beginner would be lost when sitting down with a bunch of sharks who played day in and day out and knew all the nuances and intricate rules of the game.

The games were for comparatively low stakes, ranging from $1-$2 all the way to the $15-$20 California blind, and the rentals ranged from $1 to $4 per half hour. There was no house cut, just rentals. All the clubs wanted were for their tables to be filled with players, who paid their rentals.

Now, the situation has changed entirely. In the clubs running the length and breadth of California, the legislature has seen fit to allow other poker games, such as stud and hold 'em, as well as a slew of exotic poker games with fancy names like California aces. What the legislature mandates in these clubs is that the players play against each other, never against the house. All the house does is supply a dealer and take a cut, or rake from each pot. A game like California aces is really blackjack played as a poker game. Other games are disguised baccarat games also played as poker games. These are exotic games and need not concern us here. In the clubs, they are played in special rooms, with heavy betting and gambling. The skill level has been sacrificed for the mere thrill of gambling. Since we feel that poker is primarily a game of skill, we'll write only about the games of seven card stud and hold'em, played in the clubs.

Bad Beat Jackpot

One special feature that the clubs have is the "bad beat jackpot." In both seven card stud and hold'em, if a player loses with at least aces full to a higher hand (not a higher aces full hand) he is rewarded for the bad beat. The term is self-evident. You expect to win with aces full. If you lose, you've taken a bad beating. However, the casinos reward the loser and the winner of the hand, with the loser getting the biggest share.

For example, suppose you're playing at the Commerce Club in Commerce, California, just south of Los Angeles. You're in a game of seven-card stud, a $5-$10 game, and you hold aces full. Another player holds four 7s. You both are entitled to the jackpot. As a loser, you get 75% of it and the winner of the hand gets 25%. And these jackpots aren't chopped liver. They run into the thousands of dollars. On special occasions, during some hours and weeknights, they're tripled, with payouts running to $60,000 and more.

Seven card stud makes the jackpot easier than that in hold'em. Because in hold'em not only must you have at least aces full and lose to at least four of a kind, but both players must be able to play both their hole cards. First, let's show an ideal situation for a jackpot. One player is dealt two aces and the other two 5s. The board shows:

$$\spadesuit A \; \clubsuit 5 \; \diamondsuit 5 \; \heartsuit 10 \; \clubsuit 3$$

The aces full player uses both his aces in his hand to form the best hand. The player with the pair of 5s also uses them from his hand for the best possible hand. Jackpot time!

However, suppose this occurred. One player holds ace and 10 unsuited. The other holds a pair of 8s. The board is as follows:

$$\diamondsuit A \; \heartsuit A \; \clubsuit 8 \; \diamondsuit 8 \; \spadesuit K$$

The aces full hand loses to the four 8s. But the aces full player's best possible hand is the ace from his hand combined with the two aces from the board plus the 8s. The ten in his hand is a dead card. Since he can't use both of his hole cards, there is no jackpot, just a very very bad beat.

These jackpots build up and some players have had a welcome surprise, when all the cards turn out just right for the big payout. There is another limit to jackpots, however. They are limited to the smaller games, so that anyone playing $10-$20 poker of any kind in the Commerce Casino, for instance, isn't entitled to a bad beat jackpot.

Each casino has different rules. Some vary the payouts, and some reward every player at the table. Check on the rules regarding bad beat jackpots when you play in a California club. You might as well be optimistic and prepared.

Some Nevada casinos have included this kind of jackpot, but basically, the Nevada casinos don't have jackpots, at least not in poker.

Seven Card Stud

The clubs offer a wide variety of seven card stud games, running from $1-$2 all the way to $75-$150 and sometimes higher. In all games up to $10-$20, there is an ante, and the house rake is removed prior to the dealing of the cards. In a normal $5-$10 stud game, the ante is $1 and the house removes $5 immediately from the pot, leaving $3 on the table. "Low card brings it in", that is, the low card must make the first bet for $2. For the purpose of bringing it in, suits count. If one player is dealt a deuce of clubs and another the deuce of diamonds, the club 2 must bring it in. Clubs are the lowest suit, followed by diamonds, hearts and spades.

One reason for this high rake is the jackpot, which is fed by all these antes. After a player brings in the bet for $2, the bet may be called or raised to $5. After this round of betting, we move to fourth street, where the betting is still at the $5 level unless there is an open pair, when there is an option of betting $5 or $10. Thereafter, for the remaining streets, the betting is at the $10 level.

Once the game is played for $10-$20 and up, there is a rental charged per half-hour. The rental varies from club to club, and there is an ante as well, going up in proportion to the game, encouraging faster action because of the chance of "stealing the ante," that is, raising and forcing the other players out to grab the ante.

To play successfully in the seven card games in the California clubs, you must be aggressive. Anytime you hold a premium pair, such as 10s or better, you must think of raising unless there are three other cards behind you of higher valuation. In the smaller games, there are many free cards given, with players checking all the way to the river unless they feel they have the absolute best hand or nuts.

You can't afford to play that way. Make the others pay if you feel you have the best hand. If the other players look as if they have drawing hands, by all means bet. Don't give them a free ride so that they can beat you as cheaply as possible. Make them pay.

In the clubs, play in smaller games to get your feet wet. You can find all kinds of cheap games, but I would suggest you start with at least $3-$6 or $5-$10. If you play according to our suggestions in the section on seven card stud, you should be able to handle these players with ease. By being aggressive, you'll make them uncomfortable and take control of the game. Only if you can win in the smaller games, should you then go to the bigger games. Go step by step and win by win, and you won't go wrong.

Hold'em Poker

At one time, seven card stud was the most popular of the club games, but now its place has been taken by hold'em. The clubs are overrun with hold'em games. It is a better action game, and players also like it because they only have to look at one board, open to all. In seven card stud, a player has to follow each card dealt to every player remaining in the game. This is hard to do, and it is the considered opinion of players that hold'em takes less energy to play than seven card stud.

The games available range from $1-$2 all the way up to $300-$600 in the larger clubs. If the players are available for the big games, the club will accommodate them. The most popular are the smaller limit games, with a great deal of action in $3-$6 and $6-$12. All games of $10-$20 and above are not involved with the bad beat jackpot.

Very popular are the $10-$20 and the $15-$30 games. The $15-$30 is a very fast action game, and is a true test for the experienced hold'em player. After that beckons the $20-$40 and $30-$60 action games. A lot of money can be won or lost in these games, and before playing at that level, you should have been able to beat the smaller games regularly and at the same time have a substantial and sufficient bank-roll. I always suggest at least 45 times the minimum bet.

Thus, in a $3-$6 game, bring about $150 to the table. For the $6-$12 game, have $270. When we discuss a $30-$60 game, you must have $1,350 on hand. This is not chicken feed, of course, and your larger bankroll should withstand a loss, perhaps a few times in a row. Don't go into the $30-$60 game unless you have $12,000 behind you as a stake, if you are going to play that game regularly.

The smaller games, up to $10-$20, require an ante, plus two blinds. The normal ante, whether for $3-$6 or $6-$12 is 50 cents. Then there are two blinds. There will be a $1 and $3 blind for the smaller game, and a $2 and $6 blind for the bigger one. The house rake is taken off the table prior to the dealings of the cards. The rake not only gives the house its money, but puts aside money for the bad beat jackpot.

Since the dealer must remove chips and antes and set aside the rake immediately, the game is slower than the $10-$20 and bigger games, where there is no ante, just a rental collected by the half-hour. The rental varies from club to club and game to game. The bigger the game, the higher the rental. Thus, with no ante and no rake, the game proceeds much faster.

An interesting feature of hold'em is that the structure of the game never varies. There are usually two blinds and one is small and about half the larger one. In the smaller games, as we have seen, one is a bit more than double the other. In the bigger games, up to $10-$20, the big blind is double the small blind. All that is different between the smaller and bigger games is the amount of money at stake, and the quality of the players. Obviously, good players end up in bigger games, and great players play in the biggest games. There may be exceptions to this statement, but when you play a bigger game, expect stronger players.

Study our section on hold'em and practice at home. Then play in the smaller games to get your feet wet. If you continually lose, re-examine what you are doing. You may be playing too loosely.

Stick to our strategies and you should be a winner. Then, move up in class only after you beat the smaller games. It may be that you're comfortable at a certain level, either emotionally or financially. Then stick to that level, if you keep winning there.

Draw Poker

Draw poker is still available in many California clubs, but it is a dying game, with only a few tables available in the big clubs, while the place is overrun with hold'em games.

Study our section on both high and low draw poker. In the clubs, there is a joker added to the deck. In high poker this joker or "bug" has limited value. It can be used to form flushes and straights, and can also be used as an ace. Thus, the best hand at high draw in the clubs is five aces.

Most of the games are jacks or better, that is, a pair of jacks are necessary to open the betting action. The games are played with antes. It is a rather slow game for those accustomed to greater action, and that is one of the reasons for its steady precipitous decline.

Low poker played as draw poker still hangs in there in some California clubs. Like high draw, the game is usually dealt by a house dealer instead of the individual players as in past times. There is an ante and sometimes a live blind in the game. Since position counts in all draw games, a button signifies the imaginary dealer when a house dealer is employed by the casino.

If draw poker is your game, make sure that the club you're going to offers the game. Often, even if they do have the game, it may be for very low stakes, for stakes you're not interested in. The best games to make big money in when at the California clubs are hold'em and seven card stud.

11. NEVADA AND CASINO POKER

As more and more jurisdictions around the country offer gambling games, the casinos in these areas often have poker available to the patrons. They aren't at risk offering this game. It is very popular and attracts players. The casino collects its rake or its rentals and makes money. The players win and lose money among themselves. A player on a hot streak only cripples the bankrolls of other players, not the casino.

Atlantic City, after many years without poker, now has introduced it as one of its games. There is poker available at Indian reservations and at card clubs in many states. If you want a poker game, in many jurisdictions you're going to have no trouble finding one.

In Las Vegas, many casinos both on and off the Strip and downtown, offer poker games. At one time the best games downtown were offered at the Golden Nugget, but they've discontinued their poker operation and moved it to the Mirage, a sister hotel-casino. As of this writing, the Mirage offers the best games with the best players. Downtown, the Horseshoe Club, after digesting the Mint next door, has opened a big poker room.

For many years Caesars Palace had the big poker games on the Strip, but they've also closed up their poker room. Many of the dealers who originally worked at Caesars are now firmly established at the Mirage.

Let us use the Mirage as an example of a casino poker room. The Mirage offers basically two games, seven card stud and hold'em. It also, from time to time has "razz", which is seven card stud played as a low game. It also occasionally, if the players are there, has a "high-low split" game, which is high low seven card stud, in which "the cards speak". The high-low game we've discussed previously is a declare game, in which players declare whether or not they're going high or low, or "pigging it", going both ways.

In the casino game of high-low split, the cards are turned over by the players at the showdown, and the winning hands are then declared by the dealer. The rule of cards speaking probably prevents a great many arguments. There is no declaring by the players. If a player wins both ways, his cards show it, and he "scoops the pot". In other words, he takes the whole pot.

Another game we should mention, that is also played in the California clubs, is Omaha 8 or Better. This is a variant of hold'em, where each player is dealt four cards instead of the two dealt in hold 'em. Players can only use two of their cards from their hand to form the best hand. Like hold'em, there is a flop, then the turn and river, with five cards on board. By 8 or Better, we mean that there is also a low winning hand, but it must be 8 or below. For example an 8 6 5 4 2 is a valid low hand. A 9 4 3 2 Ace is not a valid low hand.

In order to have a low hand, at least three cards on board must be 8 or below, because each player must use two of his cards to form any hand. Therefore, the best low cards to hold in your hand is Ace-2, preferably suited, so that you can go after the high flush, as well.

With the two-card rule, a hand holding four of a kind in the hole isn't very good, because all a player can do is use one pair of these four matched cards. Because of the high-low nature of this game, you can use two cards in your hand for the low hand and two others for the high hand. For example, suppose you hold the following: ♣3 ♣5 ♦J ♠J

The board shows:

♣A ♥6 ♠4 ♥J ♦6

You can use your 3 and 5 to form a low of 6-5, and you can also use your pair of jacks to form a full house, jacks over 6s.

The game is played with one or two blinds. There is a button that moves around the table signifying the imaginary dealer, because, like hold'em, position is important. Dealers dislike the game, because practically all winning hands are split, and the dealers must divide up the chips correctly. In the other games, for the most part, all the chips are shoved to the winning player.

In larger casinos with popular poker rooms, the stud games usually start at $1-$4 and move up to the stratosphere. I've seen a no limit stud game played there, with several immortals of the game participating. It had started as a measly $2,000-$4,000 game and worked its way up after a few days.

In the stud games, there is an ante, and the ante increases disproportionately as the games get bigger. For example, in a $10-$20 game, the ante is $1, but in the $100-$200 game, the ante moves up to $25. This larger ante structure makes for a "faster" game, that is, a game in which there is more betting on third street, for the ante is an important consideration and adds up.

If you try your hand at stud in a casino, try and avoid the $1-$4 games, in which the rake can add up to 25% in some places. Start at the $5-$10 game, which usually has a limit of $2.50 taken out as a rake. If you succeed in the smaller games, you can move up to the bigger games. The dividing line is the $15-$30 game which attracts local pros. This game is the first of the rental games in stud, in which you pay the house by the half-hour to play.

Hold'em is very popular and sports more tables than seven card stud in most casinos. In some Las Vegas casinos, there are two blinds in all the hold'em games, but no ante. Thus, the game moves quite fast, and is cheaper to play than a comparable game in the California clubs, where the antes do add up. Of course, there is no bad beat jackpot either, so if you're in a low level game and lose with four of a kind to a bigger four of a kind, its just tough, a bad beat without any compensation.

Hold'em may start at $1-$2, though in some casinos, the cheapest game is $3-$6 and it moves up from there. You can play $6-$12, $10-$20, and so forth. The blind structure is always in proportion, and if you can beat a $20-$40 game, you are a good player. Again, play within your limits, both emotionally and financially and you won't get hurt. Try the smaller games before going to the bigger ones, and move up only if you can beat the smaller games.

In the casinos and California clubs there is a buy-in, a certain amount you must sit down with to play. The games are table stakes as well. You cannot pull out more money from your pocket in the course of playing a hand. However, you can keep cash on the table. In the California clubs, any denomination is usually ok. In the Nevada clubs, some limit the cash to $100 bills. Check with the dealer if in doubt. You don't want to get a monster hand only to run out of money to bet.

In the Nevada and other casinos, but not in the California clubs, you can order liquor from a waitress. But my best advice is this - don't drink. It'll affect your judgment and you have to keep a clear head when playing. If you watch the pros at play, they never drink while gambling. Never. They're winners. Learn from them. Don't drink and play.

12. Psychological Aspects of Poker

A word that is often used in poker is "courage." A player must have courage, the experts say, but they rarely define what they mean by it. Everyone has his or her definition of that word, but how does it apply to poker?

It has been my experience that in order to have courage in any endeavor in life, one must have the requisite knowledge of the particular situation in which courage is called for.

To attack a man who is holding a gun aimed at you is not courage. It is reckless stupidity because your knowledge should prepare you for the fact that in a tenth of a second a trigger can be squeezed and a bullet hurtled at tremendous speed into your body, doing irreparable harm and possibly causing death.

To act courageously in that situation might simply be to act without panic, to protect those who are with you by not cringing in fear.

Another example. The leopard is a beautiful, sleek animal, full of power and grace, but when it sees the lion feeding in the open, it backs off and stays in the forest. This is not to say anything against the leopard. The courage of the leopard is not at stake here at all.

The leopard knows that if he challenges the lion to the feeding ground, the leopard might be maimed, or worse, killed by the lion. No animal is a match for the lion on those terms. So the leopard retreats and goes about his business.

The leopard has his own courage, and if lions are in the vicinity it doesn't mean that it will not go there. It will not confront the lion, however, head to head. Again, I repeat, this has nothing to do with courage. For the leopard to challenge the lion under these conditions would again be reckless stupidity.

The same rules hold true in life and in poker. In many ways anyone reading this book can see that the two are not that dissimilar and that at a poker table you often see a man or woman open and exposed in a way he or she wouldn't dare to be in life.

We see the bluffer, the complainer, the loser, the winner, the cunning player, the stupid player, the tight and loose players; we see all kinds of people, and we can categorize them fairly quickly at the table. A strong player doesn't become a weak player in the course of an evening, and neither does a tight player become a loose player.

A weak player going after all the pots isn't suddenly transformed into a brilliant, shrewd player. No, the players, by this point in their lifetime, bring to the poker table a lifetime of habits and thinking, and we can pretty well judge them as poker players. Since money is at stake, emotions tend to run high, and when emotions and feelings are open, the psychological aspects of the game become very important and can be used to advantage by a knowledgeable player in much the same way he can use his knowledge of the odds and strategy.

To go back to courage. It is not courage to chase two aces with two kings, making an enormous bet and praying for that third cowboy. That is, again, reckless stupidity. But many players mix up the two, thinking that tight players are timid players, and that the courageous ones are those who are in all the pots, taking the raises and reraises with their chins up while waiting for their inside straights or their three flushes to develop, or chasing superior cards with their inferior ones, hoping for some miracle.

What is courage, then, at the poker table? It is the ability to take control of a situation and to be bold when the situation calls for it. If you have the table beaten, and there is one more card to buy, then you must have the courage to make a big bet and force the weaker hands to drop out or to call your bet at a disadvantage.

When you don't have courage in a game, it weakens your play. The game of poker is not for the timid; it is for the bold. I keep using the word "bold," and I think this is what many of the experts and great players talk about when they use the word courage.

Another aspect of courage is the ability to absorb bad breaks and losses and not alter your style of play. For example, you might have lost a few big pots with a full house to a higher full house or with good hands that somehow were beaten. Now is the test of your courage. Again, you have a good hand, a very strong hand that can win the pot, and you seem to have everyone beaten on board. To have courage in this situation is to bet the limit, to push that pot all the way up, to push your cards as far as they'll go.

If you start thinking of the previous losing hands and the previous losses, and you check or make a small bet, then you're not being bold; you are said to "lack courage".

The higher the limits, the more psychology plays a part in poker. In a limit game, particularly a small - or medium-limit game, the play is generally tight because there is hardly any way for any player to bluff another using money. Position alone can be used as a psychological pressure.

When the game goes into higher limits, into $100 and higher bets, into pot-limit games and no-limit games, then we have another story altogether. Not only do the cards and position now play a big role, but money itself. When you have both money and position on the table, you can easily use them as psychological bludgeons.

For example, suppose in a pot-limit game in high draw poker you were the dealer, and you raised the pot before the draw and then drew one card.

There are two players remaining with you. After the draw, both check; you count the pot and push in the pot's total as your bet.

You've used your money and your superior position at this moment. The other players are at a disadvantage. You drew one card and now are betting the limit. They don't know what you have. Would you raise on a four flush or four straight? Not likely. Perhaps you are holding two high pair, three of a kind, or maybe four of a kind.

Or maybe you're holding nothing. You may be bluffing, but the other players are in a bad spot to call, especially since you made a big raise before drawing a card.

Remember, having the position and money scares the hell out

of other players. They have to make an educated guess about your hand, they have to try to "read" your hand, and that puts them at a tremendous disadvantage. You've made your bet, and you sit back. If you don't give your hand away ("tell" your hand), you're in a beautiful spot.

There's nothing worse than sitting with three kings on the fourth round of betting, making a bet, and then watching the holder of a pair of aces showing raise you the limit in a game of seven-card stud, high, pot limit. There you are, trying to guess if the raiser has the third ace. This ability to gauge hands, to guess or read a hand, separates the big winners from the losers.

The very top players have an uncanny ability to read hands. They study the opponents, they watch their gestures, movements, and mannerisms, looking for the "tell," for the one thing that gives the hand away.

A player who is bluffing and betting a large amount is often like a guilty man taking a lie detector test. He may think he's outwardly calm, but a lot of barely noticeable things are giving him away. His heart will be pounding, the pulse in his neck or temple will be beating at a strong, fast pace, his hands will be shaking, his voice will chage in tone and pitch. All these things are giveaways, and they are watched by experts.

I watch other things as well. Before I call a big raise, I keep my eyes on the raiser's face. Is he pleased that I'm calling the raise? Is he nervous? A smile can go both ways, and once, calling a pot-limit bet, my opponent smiled, but the corners of his lips were trembling. I called, then raised the limit. He folded his cards.

If, on the other hand, he was happy to see my bet, if that smile was genuine and not one of anxiety, I would have thrown in my cards. But his mouth was trembling, and a man with a lock on the game doesn't tremble.

Even great players, like the former world champion of hold'em poker, Doyle Brunson, had a "tell." I watched him play at the Horseshoe. He generally keeps a downcast face, a sullen noncommittal expression on his face, a perfect poker face. When shoving in all his chips on one hand, he looked sullen and showed no affect.

But in an interview for a gambling magazine, Doyle mentioned that "Amarillo Slim" Preston pointed out to him at one time that he knew when he was bluffing. He knew because when Doyle bluffed, he moved in all his chips without counting them, and when he wasn't bluffing, he counted his chips before shoving them in.

As I mentioned at the beginning of this section, courage is tied up with knowledge. If you know the odds in poker, if you know that you have advantage, then you have to go the limit with that knowledge and be bold. You can't play scared.

I was in a big game of seven card stud, high-low. I was out of this particular hand, but a big loser showed three 10s, with two cards still to buy. He had been beaten out of a few big pots through careless betting and poor judgment, and now, probably remembering those unhappy hands, he fingered his chips with uncertainty and checked.

Heavy sighs were heard. Everyone checked on that round. A player holding two jacks bought a third one and took command. As a result of the player's lack of courage, he lost his share of the pot for the high hand to the three jacks and would have probably forced out that hand with a big bet before the third jack was bought.

He lacked confidence, and thus courage. You must feel confident when you sit down to play poker; otherwise, get out of the game. Now it is perfectly normal to feel an inner tension in a high-stakes game of poker. That is natural, and that slight tension keeps one on his toes.

But confidence is another matter. You must feel you can beat the group you're playing with. You must feel you know what you're doing, that you have, in fact, superior knowledge of tactics and strategy. You must feel that you're going to win, period. That's confidence.

The way to win at poker is to win money, not necessarily pots. I've seen bad players win a lot of pots because they bought good cards, but they were losers in the end, and I've seen superior players win money while taking only a couple of pots all evening. What was the difference? The smart players made sure they built big pots for themselves, and the weak players didn't. The difference was control, a tremendous factor in psychological poker.

If you have the top cards, you must take control of the game and build the pot according to your cards. With cards that will win without any help in the buy or draw, you want to keep everyone in the pot, contributing. With hands that are strong but that might be beaten by a lucky buy or draw, you want to force out the opposition and make the weaker hands pay heavily to stay in.

In most games the one or two strongest players take control of the game and run it. The other players fear them, fear the raises and the pace of the game. Games are controlled by superior players not by weak players, no matter how good their holdings. The point is: Try to be the one controlling the pace, force the game to your needs, and don't be passive.

And there, in three words, is what the heart of psychological poker is all about: courage, knowledge, and control. With these three factors going for you, working for you, you'll be hard to beat in any game, for any stakes.

13. BLUFFING

Bluffing may be defined as betting heavily on a weak hand to mislead an opponent. If the bluff succeeds, the opponent drops out, and you win the pot with inferior cards. The bluff fails if the opponent calls your bet or, worse, reraises you, forcing you to drop out.

Bluffing is an important aspect of the game of poker and comes into play because some or all of the cards of each hand are hidden and therefore unknown. Even a single hidden card can turn the trick, as in a game like five-card stud, particularly if it is a check-and-raise game.

Suppose you hold Q K 4 3 A, the queen being hidden. Your opponent holds * J 10 9 5. You've figured him for jacks wired from the beginning, and he's bet as if he had them. When you bought the 3 on the fourth card, you checked, and he made a big bet, which you called.

On the last card you check again, he makes a big bet, and suddenly you go all out with a huge raise. He is now in a terrible position, which he put himself in by being greedy. Since only the two of you were in the game at the showdown, he might as well have checked also and been content to take whatever the pot had to offer.

Now he is in a real bind. The best he can have is jacks because if he has merely an ace in the hole, he's beaten on board. Now he has to think that you've been playing possum and going along quietly with a pair of kings wired, or possibly that the ace has finally paired up with another ace in the hole. The one hole card, in this instance, has made the bluff a very powerful weapon. It would be very difficult for him to call your bluff in a high-limit game.

Three factors enter into every bluffing situation. They are: (1) your opponent: (2) your position at the table; (3) the stakes you are playing for.

We'll try and deal with each one separately, but in many ways they are all interdependent on one another.

First, let's discuss our opponents. The easiest player to bluff is a strong, tight player, believe it or not. This kind of player is not afraid of being bluffed out of a hand and will respect a big raise.

On the other hand, a weak player is continually going after cards that he hopes will improve his hand, and it is immaterial to him whether or not you hit him with a big raise. In his way of thinking, which of course is backwards, he figures that you are building up a bigger pot for his inside straight, when he hits it.

It's very difficult to bluff out a weak player, but a bluff may work in certain situations. The weak player must be a loser, and a big loser at that, before he becomes susceptible to a bluff. If you try to bluff out a weak player who is a winner, you are asking for trouble. He will take a lot of punishment to stay in to the show-down.

Many players, however, are neither very weak nor very strong. They're mediocre players who neither chase pots with reckless abandon nor stay in pots only when they have the edge. How do you deal with them in terms of bluffing?

Here position and money are important considerations. The bigger the stakes, the easier it is to bluff, especially in those games in which there is a pot limit or no limit. You can use your money in those games in the same manner that you use skill in limit games.

A "pot-limit game" is one in which a player can bet or raise the entire pot. If there is $100 in the pot, he can bet $100 and raise $100. This makes the game much different from an ordinary $10-$20 game. Here a player can bet $20 or raise that same amount, and that's it. Anyone can call that $20 bet. But when you can really throw in money, the whole situation changes.

In any case, it is easier to bluff out a big loser than a big winner. When you are against a player who is nervously fingering his chips, who has been losing steadily and is now counting what he has left, and you make a bet that is equal to his remaining stake, your money alone has him over the barrel. Your money and his lack of money may decide if the bluff will work.

On the other hand, if you're up against a big winner, he may decide to call the bluff. He may feel, no matter how mediocre a player he is, that everything has been going well for him, that he is on a hot streak, a tear, and that nothing can go wrong.

Besides money, position is just as important. By "position" I mean the relative placing of players at a table. If you bet behind a player, that is, after him, you have an advantage in all poker games, but especially in draw poker, in which all the cards are concealed.

Let's assume that in high draw poker, anything opens, you are left at the showdown with one other player after the draw. You are behind him, and after he drew one card, you drew two.

Prior to the draw, when he opened, you raised him, and he called the raise. There is $100 in the pot, and the game is pot limit.

He picks up his one card and checks. You had raised on a pair of kings and held another high card, a queen as a kicker only for strategic purposes. When he didn't reraise you, you figured him for a pair, but he took only one card, and now you figure him for two pair, perhaps a middling pair headed by jacks or 10s, but there's now way of knowing. In any event, you would think that if he had aces up going in, he could have reraised you at the outset.

There's only one reason to draw two cards and hold the stupid queen. That's because, having position on him, you've seen him first draw one card. If you drew three cards, he'd have control of the game, and he could then bet big, figuring that he had you beat going in to the draw. The two-card draw had kept you in control.

He must now figure you for three of a kind. By drawing those two cards, you have impressed this upon him, along with your raise. You have position on him and can augment the position with a money bet. You first look at your cards. As expected, you haven't improved.

You count the pot and bet and raise the whole pot, putting in $200. Your opponent is now in an awful fix. He's going to have to drop those two pair. If he calls, he'll be trembling and feel like an utter fool. He already feels he's beaten. Why else would you raise and then draw two cards if you didn't have three of a kind?

If your opponent had wanted to keep control, he should have bet the pot after looking at his drawn card, but it's 11-1 against him drawing to improve two pair, and he knows you know this. He checked, hoping you'd check also or make a small bet. If he had bet the pot, he might have been bluffing without position, and if you came back with a big raise, he'd be in the same bind, or a worse one if he hadn't improved his two pair.

These money and position situations come up time and time again in poker. You can take advantage of them and learn from them. When you are not in good position, either be supercautious, or do the bluffing by taking the initiative.

Suppose you are under the gun and open the betting in high draw poker, then are raised, then you reraise. On the draw you're in a terrible position since you're first to draw, but you decide to stand pat. You now have retained control, and if you go in with a big bet (and you have to, or they'll see through your bluff), you've put the other players to the wall. But it takes a lot of courage and the ability to keep control and not give away the bluff.

When you're playing head to head with a weak player, if he has position on you, and you have mediocre cards, it's best to fold. You probably won't be able to bluff him out, and you won't win with the best hand. So what's the use of staying in? Save your big bets for the times you have the real goods, and then sock it to him.

In situations in which I suspect other players of bluffing, I look for mannerisms or gestures that give away their bluff. These are known as "tells."

Are their hands shaking when they put in the big bet? Have their voices changed? Are they swallowing hard? Are they very nervous, very anxious? I watch them carefully for any tell.

When I bluff, I try to avoid any tells on my behalf and try to play each hand in the same way. When I'm making any kind of bet, whether large or small, I try to do it in the same manner.

Perhaps I do give myself away. I don't know, but I don't think so. I've practiced before mirrors to get the same blank look on my face on any bet, large or small. It pays to practice this way in front of a mirror to really see what your face looks like when you're bluffing.

In limit games, even small-limit games, it's possible to bluff but much more difficult, and I use bluffing in these games sometimes to steal a pot with inferior cards or sometimes just to lose a small pot on purpose. I want the other players to feel that I don't play as tight a game as they think I do.

So in these makes I wait for the right bluffing situations. I wait for a small pot with only one or two players in with me; then I raise and try to drive them out with a bluff. If they call my raise, I turn over my cards to show I was bluffing. On future raises, when I really have the goods, I'm going to get some of them in with me, perhaps even reraising me.

One session I played in a Nevada casino was very profitable when I used this method. I had bluffed on a few pots and been called on each one, showing my weak cards even though I didn't have to. Then I developed a wonderful hand of three jacks full, with two of the jacks as hole cards, dealt immediately.

I raised throughout and was reraised. On the last betting round there were five raises, the limit, before I was called. When I put down those three jacks full, my opponents were stunned, and that pot repaid me tenfold for all my previous small bluffs.

To sum up: It's easier to bluff strong players than weak players. It's easier to bluff out a big loser than a big winner. The bigger the stakes, the easier it is to bluff. Money and position are important considerations, as are the opponents.

Before bluffing, remember the three factors involved: opponent, money, and position. Have at least two of these factors, preferably all three, on your side when you decide to bluff.

Finally, use the bluff to your advantage at times to give the impression that you're not as tight or strong a player as the others at the table feel you are. It'll pay off in spades for you.

GLOSSARY

The following are explanations of terms and phrases used in poker:

Aces Up - A hand containing a pair of aces and another pair.

Ante - Money or chips placed into the pot prior to a deal. Also called "sweetening the pot."

Back In - Checking a strong hand and then raising after another player opens the betting when check-and-raise is permitted.

Back to Back - A holding of a pair in five-card stud, where the pair is formed on the first two cards dealt, one in the hole and the other as the first upcard. Also known as "wired."

Bad Beat - Losing with a powerful hand such as aces full.

Bad Beat Jackpot - A jackpot paid by a club or casino for a bad beat.

Bet - The amount of money or chips wagered on a single play.

Betting the Pot - In pot-limit poker, betting an amount equal to the sum of the pot.

Bicycle - In lowball and high-low poker the lowest possible holding 5 4 3 2 A. Also called a "wheel."

Big Blind - The bigger of two forced bets in a game such as hold'em.

Blind - A forced bet before the cards are dealt.

Blind Bet - A forced bet that is mandatory without regard to the value of the holdings. In some variations of poker the first player to act, the one "under the gun", must make a blind bet.

Bluffing - Betting on an inferior hand with the intention of misleading the other players so that they drop out of the game.

Board - The five community cards dealt open in hold'em or Omaha.

Bonus - An extra payment for holding outstanding hands, such as a royal flush or straight flush. Also called "royalties".

Bring it in - Making a forced bet in a stud game, thus opening the betting.

Bull - A common slang term for the ace.

Burn a Card - Discarding the top card of a stock or deck before dealing.

Bust - A terrible hand, having no chance to win.

Button - When there is a house dealer, usually in casino poker, a button is put in front of a player to signify that he is the theoretical dealer, so that he bets and acts last. The button is moved around the table in consecutive clockwise order.

Buy; Buy a Card - To receive a card during a round of stud poker.

Call; Call a Bet - To make a bet equal to a previous bet on the same round. Also called "seeing a bet."

Calling a Hand - Making a final bet in order to see the original bettor's hand at the showdown.

Cards Speak - The cards shown determine the winner of a pot, rather than any declaration by a player.

Case Card - The last card of a particular rank. If a player buys a jack after three have shown, he is said to have bought the "case jack."

Check - The act of "not betting" and passing the bet option to the next player while still remaining an active player, Players cannot check when a bet has been made. Also called "Pass".

Check-And-Raise - When allowed, a player may check his hand, and then raise a subsequent bet when it is his turn again.

Connected Suited Cards - A holding such as the 8-9 of spades.

Cowboy - A slang term for the king.

Cut; Cut the Cards - The player to the dealer's right removes the top part of the deck and puts it to one side after the cards have been shuffled by the dealer. Then the dealer puts the bottom part on top of the other part and squares the deck prior to dealing.

Deadwood - The discard pile; cards folded by the players or discarded prior to the draw.

Deuce - A common term for the 2.

Discard Pile - See Deadwood.

Draw - Cards dealt from the stock after the first betting round in draw poker is over.

Drawing Hand - A hand that needs improvement to win, such as a four-flush.

Drop - To go out of the game or "fold one's cards."

Face Card - The jack, queen, or king.

False Opener's - In jackpots, in which jacks or better are necessary to open the betting, the opening of the betting by a player with an inferior and thus, inadequate hand.

Fifth Street - See River.

Fill In - To draw or buy cards that improve the player's orginal holding.

Flop - The first three cards placed on the board after the first betting round is over in hold'em.

Flush - A hand containing five cards of one suit.

Fold - To drop out of the game by throwing in or discarding one's holding.

Four Flush - An insufficient holding of four cards of one suit, not enough for a flush.

Four of a Kind - See Turn.

Fourth Street - The fourth card put on board in hold'em, which begins the third round of betting.

Free Card - Getting to see another card without having to bet.

Free Ride - A round in which all the players pass, and there's no betting.

Full House - A holding consisting of three of a kind and a pair. Example: 8 8 8 3 3.

High - In stud poker, the highest-ranking card on board, whose holder makes the first bet.

High Hand - The highest-ranking hand in high poker for a particular game.

Hole Card - In stud poker a card or cards dealt face down.

Inside Straight - A four straight shy a card in the interior of the sequence, such as 7 6 - 4 3.

Jackpots - A variation of draw poker, in which a holding of a pair of jacks or better is necessary to open the first round of betting.

Joker Wild - Any poker game in which the joker's used as a wild card.

Kicker - A high card, usually an ace or king, held with a lower-ranking pair for the draw in draw poker.

Limit - The maximum bet that can be made or raised.

Live Blind - A blind that can be raised when it is the blind's turn to act.

Nuts - A powerful hand that cannot be beaten in any particular game. This term is often used in hold'em.

Offsuit - Cards not of the same suit.

Open; To Open - Making the first bet on the first betting round.

Open-Ended Straight - A holding of four cards in sequence in which any outside card bought or drawn would make the hand a straight. Example: - 9 8 7 6 - .

Openers - In jackpots the cards that were used to open the betting, that is, a pair of jacks, or better.

Pass - See Check.

Pat Hand - In draw poker a five-card holding is a made hand even without a draw, such as a straight or flush.

Pigging it - Declaring both high and low in a high-low game.

Pocket Cards - The two cards dealt face down to a player in hold'em.

Pot - The total amount of money and chips, including the ante, previously bet during the game.

Pot Limit - A betting limit in which the total of the pot can be bet by a player as a single bet.

Pot Odds - The odds the pot will offer a player for his bet.

Raise - A bet larger than the previous one, which must be met by all the players in the game on that betting round.

Rake - The cut the house takes out of a pot in casino poker.

Razz - A popular name for seven-card stud, lowball.

River, The River - The last card dealt in a game of stud or hold'em.

Royalties - See Bonus.

Scare Cards - Open cards that look extremely powerful to the opponents.

See A Bet - See Call.

Showdown - The showing of hands after the last bets have been made to determine the winner of the pot.

Shy - Making an inadequate bet or owing money to the pot.

Small Blind - The smaller of two forced bets in a game like hold'em.

Sweeten the Pot - See Ante.

Table Stakes - A betting limit in which a player cannot bet more than the money he has on the table and cannot, after that sum is depleted, bring out more money during that particular hand.

Tell - A mannerism by which a player gives away the value of his hole card or his hand.

Turn, The Turn - Fourth Street in a stud game or the fourth card on the board in hold'em.

Under the Gun - The player to the dealer's left who is forced to act or bet first in any betting round.

Wheel - The best hand in lowball. See Bicycle.

Wired - See Back to Back.

Wild Card - A card, usually a joker or a deuce, that can have any rank or suit the holder of that card wishes to place on it.

CARDOZA PUBLISHING POKER BOOKS

WINNING POKER FOR THE SERIOUS PLAYER *Edwin Silberstang.* 12 hard hitting chapters and more than a 100 actual examples provide tons of winning advice for beginning and advanced players at 7 Card Stud, Texas Hold 'Em, Draw Poker, Loball, High-Low and more than 10 other variations. Silberstang analyzes all the essential principles necessary to be a great poker player; when to be aggressive, when to slow play, when to fold, how to cause players to fear your bets, how to read tells, how to analyze a table, how to master the art of deception, how to play position, psychological tactics, expert plays and much more. Colorful glossary of poker terms included. 224 pages, $12.95

CARO'S FUNDAMENTAL SECRETS OF WINNING POKER *Mike Caro.* The world's foremost poker theoretician and strategist presents the essential strategies, concepts, and secret winning plays that comprise the very foundation of winning poker play. Shows how to win more from weak players, equalize stronger players, how to bluff a bluffer, where to sit against weak players, how to win big pots, the six factors of strategic table image. Includes selected tips on hold 'em, 7 stud, 7 stud high-low, five card draw, lowball, tournament play, more. 160 Pages, $9.95

COMPLETE GUIDE TO WINNING HOLD'EM POKER *Ken Warren.* The most comprehensive and powerful book on beating hold'em, shows players how to play every hand from every position with every type of flop. Players learn the 14 categories of starting hands, advantages of betting last, how to play against loose and tight players, the 10 most common Hold'em tells, how to evaluate a game for profit, the value of deception and art of bluffing, eight secrets to winning, categories of starting hands, position, and more! Bonus: Includes a painstakingly analysis of the top 40 Hold'em hands and most complete chapter on hold'em odds in print. *Fabulous* book. 224 Pages, $14.95

HOW TO PLAY WINNING POKER *Avery Cardoza.* A massive dose of easy-to-read information is jam-packed into this concise primer for beginning players. In 12 fast-reading chapters, players learn the basics of play for the most popular poker games and how to beat them using Cardoza's 5 winning strategies. Players learn how to recognize good cards, read opponent's playing styles, play position, use pot odds, find tells, and more. 96 pages, $6.95

HANDBOOK OF WINNING POKER *Edwin Silberstang.* New revision presents the latest strategies for over 10 poker variations including draw poker (jackpots, anything opens), high stud poker (5 and 7 card), low poker (5 card draw, 5 and 7 card stud, casino razz), high-low (5 and 7 card stud). The rules and strategies of winning are shown for home and casino variations, along with special chapters covering California games, Nevada casino poker, world championship play, bluffing, and psychological aspects of winning. 160 pages, $9.95

ADVANCED POKER BOOKS - OTHER PUBLISHERS

THE THEORY OF POKER *By David Sklansky.* 25 powerful chapters cover the theories and concepts of beating 5-card draw, low draw, 7-stud high and low (razz), plus hold'em. Analyzes poker hands from ante structure until showdown: You learn to think like a pro. Covers bluffing, semi-bluffing, slow-play, deception, pot odds, position, raising strategy, implied odds, free cards, reading hands, big pot play, stealing antes, psychology, hourly win rate, and much more. A **must-have** for poker players. 276 pages, $29.95.

WINNING CONCEPTS IN DRAW AND LOWBALL *By Mason Malmuth.* Written for both novices and pro players, Malmuth shows how to play and think like a pro. Covers basic and advanced strategy, technical plays, killing pots, lowball value betting, profitable losing bets, pattern plays, "running bad", raising with weak hands, bluffing errors, basic mistakes, table talk, plus powerful winning strategems to beat any type of table. 220 pages, $24.95.

POKER ESSAYS *By Mason Malmuth.* A wealth of winning concepts, strategies and technical ideas presented in a variety of short essays, shows players how to improve at hold'em and stud variation. Players learn how to evaluate opponents, analyze games, play an image, play tournament strategy, and more. 262 pages, $24.95.

Use coupon on following page for ordering or charge toll-free: (800)577-WINS

SEVEN CARD STUD FOR ADVANCED PLAYERS *By Sklansky, Malmuth, Zee.* This definitive book on 7-card stud discusses important concepts of winning: out-cards, ante stealing, playing little, medium and big pairs, 3-flushes and straights, re-raising bigger pairs, pairing door cards, advanced ante play, scare card strategy, tight, loose and short-handed strategy, and much more. Learn how to make money at seven card stud. 220 pages, $29.95.

SKLANSKY ON POKER *By David Sklansky.* New edition combines two books, *Sklansky on Razz* and *Essays on Poker*, plus new material including tournament play. Shows overall strong strategiec winning concepts including 3 levels of expert poker, middle round strategy, protecting pots, bankroll plans, saving last bets; razz section includes concepts valuable for all poker forms, rules of play, game structure, opening concepts, problem plays, 3rd-7th street strategy, expert moves. 215 pages, $29.95.

HIGH-LOW-SPLIT FOR ADVANCED PLAYERS *By Ray Zee.* Comprehensive book by a top pro player on 7 stud and Omaha 8-or-Better - really two books in one. Details tons of winning concepts; starting hands, disguising play, position, bluffing, high and low hand play, scare cards, staying to the end, analyzing opponents, how to handle raises, how to increase winnings, and much more. Includes colorful glossary. 333 pages, $34.95.

HOLD 'EM POKER FOR ADVANCED PLAYERS *By Sklansky and Malmuth.* This powerful book, among the finest on winning money at hold'em poker, covers first two card play, playing pair flops and trash hands, short-handed and head-on strategy, inducing bluffs, semi-bluffing, position play, check-raising, loose/tight play, more. 212 pages, $29.95.

HOLD 'EM POKER *By David Sklansky.* This classic hold'em manual shows beginning and intermediate players the basic winning concepts. Topics include position, key flops, first two cards, reading hands, semi-bluffing, pre-flop and post-flop strategy, slow-playing and more. Includes Sklansky Hand Rankings. 63 Pages, $17.50.

THREE MORE UNIQUE PRODUCTS!

CARO'S POWER POKER SEMINAR - $39.95
VHS Videocassette

In this **powerful** video, the world's foremost authority on poker strategy, psychology, and statistics shows you how to **win big money** with the **little-known** concepts used by great poker players and world champions. The advice here will be worth thousands of dollars to you every year, even more if you're a big money player!

Finally, after 15 years of refusing to allow his seminars to be filmed, Caro takes you on the inside track, and presents an entertaining but serious coverage of his long-guarded winning secrets. This tape contains the most profitable poker advice ever put on video, and is sure to take your game and winnings up one or two notches.

MIKE CARO'S POKER PROBE - $69.95
Powerful Poker Software for IBM-Compatibles

We now stock this software! Previously hard-to-find, this is the advanced research tool used by researchers, professional players, and poker writers to do serious work in forming optimal playing strategies at almost any form of poker. Compare hands and situations in Texas hold'em, five and seven card stud, draw poker, lowball, razz, and high-low split Omaha, to see the best way to play the cards and maximize winning results.

Power rating estimates relative value of any hand against any other, and even makes comparisons against up to 10 players! Charts howing exact odds on any two-handed "insurance" problem along with pull down menus and printable results round out a valuable piece of software. Recommended for serious poker players.

SHUFFLE TRAK™ - $79.95

(IBM-Compatible only - Requires Hard Drive, 640K Memory)
This **incredible program** is the only software which allows you to map and follow cards in a shuffle! Great for gaining advantages in blackjack, poker, baccarat - any game which uses a deck of cards - *Shuffle Trak* allows you to follow the progression of a card or segment of cards as they get shuffled in a deck. Set up zone, criss-cross, stepladder, multi-pass and other shuffle routines, and up to 9 card piles to define the shuffle. Save all shuffle patterns, and reopen at any time. *Amazing!*

This new version 5.0 also comes with Tactical Practice module which allows you to practice against any selected shuffle., and sets up automatic simulations against 7 players to examine card flow and patterns.

AVERY CARDOZA'S POKER CHAMPION

THE WORLD'S #1 TOTAL POKER EXPERIENCE & POWER TUTOR
For CD-ROM Windows - Requires 486 or better

Taking full advantage of CD-ROM Windows capabilities, this incredible 3D simulation features **four versions of poker** on **three levels** of play, beginning, average and expert, 10,000 hand-enhanced animation frames, and over **1,000 live-action voice tracks** for **21** different computer players with distinct personalities and playing styles.

STATE OF THE ART GRAPHICS/REALISTIC PLAY - Working with a $1,000,000 development budget and over a stretch of 15 months, our artists and programmers created each of the seven opponent you'll face at each level of play in 3D and integrated full-action sound and movement for completely life-like poker play.

SOPHISTICATED ARTIFICIAL INTELLIGENCE - Each opponent is **individually programmed** (84 level artificial intelligence depth) to play exactly like a real player would - your opponents call, raise, reraise and bluff. And they'll take your bluff and throw it right back in your face...unless you're good enough to stand it right back yet again. While you may learn your opponents, it doesn't mean you can beat them. *You've got to be a better player.* Be warned though, your opponents at the top level get better as the game goes on!

FLAT-OUT FUN & CHALLENGES - At each level, you take on seven opponents, each as intent on winning as you are. But to move on to higher skill levels, you must win enough money from the current table. And while you may be able to take the chumps and local yokels at Level I (the beginner's level), at the next table, the challenges are harder - it will be a battle. *If you're good enough* to move on again you'll be playing the computer world's toughest poker players. Get ready for the world's greatest poker game!

Actual Screen Shot

Each player is created in 3D, hand-enhanced, and then individually programmed with the latest artificial intelligence techniques.